the conscious kitchen

ALEXANDRA ZISSU

The New Way

to Buy and

Cook Food—

to Protect the Earth,

Improve Your Health,

and Eat Deliciously

the
conscious
kitchen

Clarkson Potter/Publishers

New York

This book is printed on 100 percent postconsumer recycled paper.

Copyright © 2010 by Alexandra Zissu

Library of Congress Cataloging-in-Publication Data
Zissu, Alexandra.
    The conscious kitchen / Alexandra Zissu. —1st ed.
       p.   cm.
    Includes index.
1. Green movement.   2. Food habits—Moral and ethical aspects.   3. Natural
foods.   4. Sustainable living.   5. Environmental responsibility.   I. Title.
    GE195.Z58   2010
    641—dc22   2009032769

ISBN 978-0-307-46140-7

Printed in the United States of America

Design by Elizabeth Rendfleisch

10   9   8   7   6   5   4   3   2   1

First Edition

To breakfast, lunch, and dinner

contents

A TALE OF TWO SATURDAYS

Saturday #1

It's a bittersweet moment when the asparagus, strawberries, and peas fade from the farmers' market and the first-of-season peaches, nectarines, blueberries, and summer squash loudly take their place. It's hard to get too wistful—corn and tomatoes are mere weeks away. Things are looking good, even for next winter, because my tiny neighborhood farmers' market has added some diverse and lovely new vendors who will be here year-round, supplying cheese, maple syrup, tender salad greens (oh, the sunflower sprouts!) and perfect pastured eggs—even in brutal and unkind February. Other new additions include farmed trout (smoked, too) and Long Island wines. Just a few years ago, I always had to supplement at the supermarket on the way home from this market. No longer. And the place is hopping! People seem, for the most part, to have their own reusable bags! A neighbor and I stop to exchange news of a butcher who come fall will open shop nearby with grass-fed and local offerings. My bags—and heart—full, I head home to add my bounty to my already farm-share-stuffed fridge. I'm elated, hopeful. I can't wait to eat lunch.

Saturday #2

We're spending the weekend away at the beach—impromptu. Although we often bring some of our food with us when traveling, we haven't this time, and our preschooler is getting cranky-hungry. I walk into a supermarket the size of a football field and easily lose an hour, dazed by choice, reading label after ingredient list after label, and further dazed that despite the monumental amount of offerings, I'm finding few conscious choices at all. People pass me pushing carts piled high with packaged, processed foods, shrink-wrapped family packs of industrially raised chicken parts, cases of bottled water. I pause before the fish counter and am amazed by the international seafood scene announced by the country-of-origin labels (COOL) (see page 30)—Sri Lanka, China, Chile—even though we're a mile or so from the Atlantic Ocean. I make do and leave. I am depressed and discouraged.

· · ·

These food highs and lows hit me often. I get all excited about the wonderful advances that are being made in the eco-food arena, and about how large the movement seems to be growing—the Obamas have an organic garden on the South Lawn! What could be huger than that?—only to be slapped back to reality. Ecologically farmed and raised food isn't widely available; the movement is too small, and often misunderstood. But it desperately needs to grow bigger—for human health and the health of the planet. As the following chapters explain, the conventional food supply that most Americans have easiest access to on a daily basis—in supermarkets, cafeterias, fast food restaurants, and takeout spots—is largely unregulated, woefully contaminated, and generally not good for us, the farmers that raise it, or the earth. There should be nothing wrong with that chicken and water—both are ostensibly healthy choices—but for many reasons, there is. We need an education to know what's going on with our food. Not enough of us know that our salad greens and chickens are being dunked in chlorine baths to disinfect them (see page 64), that bottled water is actually overpriced tap water shipped around the country in questionable plastic containers that taint their contents and overwhelm our landfills (see page 154), that dinner might contain genetically modified food (see page 23), that vegetables have been sprayed with probable carcinogens and possibly even chemical pesticides currently banned in the United States but still used in countries we import from, or that animals and seafood (some of them natural vegetarians) are fed animal by-products, waste, or even arsenic (see page 57), which sicken them and us. The average consumer, I've been told, doesn't know that the term "USDA organic" actually is a government-regulated standard and must be third-party certified (see page 21), while the term "natural" on any food packaging doesn't mean a thing (see page 57). It implies plenty, but there's nothing in place to prove or uphold the implication (though in 2009 the USDA began the process of defining it for meat and poultry only). Basically, use of the word "natural" is pure marketing.

This sort of education is hard to swallow, and it's also hard to come by. If we all collectively knew more about those shrink-wrapped chickens (see chapter three), we would vote very differently with our dollars. Even at my most discouraged, I believe this to be true. I'm not distracted by other people's supermarket grocery carts because I'm judging what they're buying. On the contrary. I'm trying to figure out how we all came to a point where we're willingly ingesting things we know so little about, and that are so incredibly harmful to our bodies and our earth. I'm distracted trying to figure out how to educate people in the most compelling and least off-putting way.

Because here's the thing: Our everyday food choices have the capacity to change the world. Demand influences supply. So it makes sense to choose wisely, consciously. The factory farming of cattle (and other animals) is an energy-intensive, inhumane, earth-polluting, greenhouse gas–releasing endeavor. Once you learn that, how hard is it to replace that burger with a smaller one that came from a well-treated grass-fed animal? Not very. "Buying grass-fed beef is the greatest thing we can do for the planet and it makes up for other things," says Alice Waters, chef, food activist, and godmother of all things local and organic. "Buying a hybrid car is nothing compared to eating grass-fed beef and not eating very much of it." If more people heard this sort of information, they'd be more inclined to shop smarter.

But, alas, most eaters don't know enough about the horrors of conventionally raised food to want to make the switch. Or they don't want to think about it. Or maybe they do want to think about it, and care deeply about it, and even have dog-eared copies of Michael Pollan's very dog-ear-able recent books on the subject (*Omnivore's Dilemma*, *In Defense of Food*), but still cannot figure out how—or where—to find the better versions of what is currently in their fridge. Who really has time to read sliced-bread ingredients for fifteen minutes at the supermarket on a vacation weekend, let alone during a weekly grocery run?

That's where *The Conscious Kitchen* comes in. It's my attempt to provide any eco-interested eater—from the newbie just going to her first farmers' market to the diehard looking for extra tips—with the education needed to make the best decisions in any venue, from convenience store to supermarket to farmers' market. The following pages are a road map for how to locate and make sense of the avalanche of "green" choices in the marketplace and how to make choosing the best possible items less work, not more.

Before I elaborate, a few crucial thoughts:

- **Conscious food is for everyone. It is not holier-than-any-thing, judgmental, or elitist.** In fact, it's common sense to want to purchase, support, and eat food that is healthiest for all involved. If anything, it's neighborly.

- **Conscious food can be affordable food** (see pages 22, 29, 63, and 122). It can actually save you money.
- **Embrace your kitchen.** You don't need fancy cooking skills, but you do have to be able to turn your thoughtfully sourced ingredients into meals. Also, you need to know how to substitute in-season ingredients in any recipe that calls for out-of-season items, or for items that don't grow at the same time in the same climate. The following pages have simple tips and recipes to help you do both.
- **Maintaining a conscious kitchen goes beyond food.** It involves employing energy-efficient appliances (see chapter nine), using cookware and cleaning products that don't contain carcinogens (see chapters eight and ten), having food storage containers that won't leach chemicals into your leftovers (see chapter eight), and taking waste into careful consideration (see chapter eleven).
- **Every little bit helps.** Doing any amount of what I suggest in the following pages can make a difference. No matter how far you take this personal journey, some is better than none.
- **Conscious food is better-tasting food.** Nothing beats the flavor of first-of-the-season sweet peas, crispy kirby cucumbers, and cherry tomatoes off the vine.

Keep those cherry tomatoes in mind as you rejigger how you approach, gather, cook, store, and dispose of your food. The goal of knowing how to wade through the gray areas of food shopping, or choosing a safe pan, or learning about the ins and outs of genetic modification, is ultimately the shock and delight of eating something that tastes exactly as it should. They're inextricably linked. A healthy, flavorful, local tomato and all that it stands for is well worth seeking out and defending—for you, for the person who grew it, and for the ground it was pulled from—for many years to come.

The Conscious Commandments

Before you even crack chapter one, here are ten easy things you can do today to move toward having a more conscious kitchen tomorrow.

1. Eat less meat. When eating beef, seek out and choose grass-fed. Other meat and poultry should also be carefully sourced (see chapter three).

2. Just say no to bottled water. Drink (filtered) tap instead (see page 96). This will save money, too.

3. Buy local organic or sustainably farmed fruits and vegetables. Don't forget that coffee and tea come from plants, and wine is made from grapes; choose sustainable versions (see chapter six).

4. Eat only the least contaminated sustainably harvested wild or well-sourced farmed seafood (see chapter five).

5. Always consider packaging when shopping. Choose items packed in materials you can reuse or that can be recycled in your municipality. Buy bulk items instead of overpackaged goods. Always shop with reusable bags (see page 160).

6. Cook at home. Often. And serve only on reusable dishware, not disposable. Clean with eco-friendly products (see chapter ten).

7. Avoid plastic as often as you can (see page 154).

8. Try composting, even if you live in a city or a house without a yard (see page 209).

9. Whenever possible, reduce energy use in the kitchen by choosing efficient appliances, cooking methods, and dishwashing practices; don't leave appliances plugged in when not in use; ask your electric company for alternative energy sources like wind power (see chapter nine).

10. Spread the word. Educate everyone you know. Green your office kitchen, your kids' school kitchen, your friends and relatives' kitchens. Make noise; together we can make a huge difference.

AGRIBUSINESS

While the blending of agriculture and business isn't inherently bad, this term has a pejorative connotation. It's used to refer to everything from the big corporate farms that spray the most pesticides to the agrochemical suppliers of said sprays (all among the largest benefactors of government subsidies).

ANTIBIOTICS

Not permitted by organic standards, these drugs are administered—prophylactically—to conventional animals living in overcrowded conditions to protect them from getting sick (see page 56). They are also used to treat dairy cows that have infections (some cows are given hormones to increase milk production, which makes them more susceptible to udder disease). Their overuse creates drug-resistant strains. It's a good idea to minimize exposure to antibiotics when you are able to identify the source, as they also can lurk in unexpected places. Tests conducted at the University of Minnesota showed that vegetables (even organic ones) fertilized with manure can absorb livestock antibiotics. For more on meat, poultry, and dairy terms like "grass-fed" and "natural," turn to chapter three.

BIODYNAMIC

An ecologically sound, third-party-certifiable method of agri-culture, this practice has roots in ancient farming and often goes beyond certified organic (see page 111). For more information, see the Demeter-USA.org website; they're the sole U.S. certification agent for biodynamic farms.

CARBON FOOTPRINT

This term refers to the total amount of carbon dioxide and other greenhouse gases created by actions like driving a car or generat-ing electricity. In a kitchen, the carbon footprint can be calculated in several ways. First is the impact of how a given food is grown, packaged, and transported. Second involves the impact of cooking, storing, cleaning, and disposing of said food.

CERTIFIED ORGANIC

This means slightly different things for meat, produce, and packaged foods. Basically it's food grown according to a set of government standards defined and regulated by the United States Department of Agriculture (USDA). These standards must be third-party certified. A USDA organic stamp guarantees that meat, poultry, and dairy prod-ucts are free of specified chemicals, hormones, and antibiotics, and that the animals they come from have been allowed a more reason-able lifestyle (see page 51). The most basic thing it means for produce is that no synthetic pesticides or fertilizers were administered (see page 21). Genetically modified or irradiated foods aren't permitted under organic standards. For more information see the USDA National Organic Program's website at AMS.USDA.gov/NOP.

COMMUNITY SUPPORTED AGRICULTURE (CSA)

CSA is a sustainable system wherein people purchase shares of a local farm (see page 35). CSA members provide cash to the farmers to work the land during the winter months and in turn reap a weekly portion of the bounty during the growing season. Share pickup either happens at a central location within the community or at the farm itself. Members often take turns working at the distribution site. CSA farms are often organic, but not always certified.

CONVENTIONAL
This means the opposite of organic and sustainable: farming (usually large scale) that doesn't involve alternative methods and does involve chemical pesticides.

ENVIRONMENTAL HEALTH
This phrase is used to describe how environmental factors (physical, chemical, and biological) external to humans—like pesticides sprayed on produce—affect personal health.

ENVIROVORE
A person who eats consciously solely for the environmental—not personal health—benefits is an envirovore.

FACTORY, FEEDLOT, OR CAFO FARMS
These words tend to be used interchangeably. Although they mean subtly different things, the general concept is that they're inhumane, environmentally destructive animal operations. Feedlots are manure-strewn, vegetation-free outdoor areas where conventionally raised cattle are confined to be fattened up (usually on grain, which isn't their natural diet and can sicken them) during their last few months of life before slaughter. Also called a feedyard. Cattle fed this way produce fattier meat that is not as healthful as grass-fed meat. CAFO (concentrated animal feeding operation) is a government-standardized term used for factory-style animal farms with thousands of hogs or even a hundred thousand plus chickens.

FAIR TRADE

This certification ensures workers have been treated fairly. It refers to both labor practices and wages. TransFair USA is currently the only independent certifier of fair-trade products in the United States. This label is most often found on exotics like coffee, tea, sugar, and bananas. For more information visit TransFairUSA.org.

FOOD MILES

The distance between where food is grown or produced and where it's consumed is referred to as an item's food miles. This can be used as one component in measuring a product's carbon footprint, though by itself it does not take into account if something was produced ecologically or conventionally.

FOODSHED

Locavores use "foodshed" to describe the square-mile area their local food comes from.

GENETICALLY MODIFIED ORGANISMS (GMOs) AND GENETICALLY MODIFIED (GM) FOOD

These terms refer to plants and their resulting crops that contain artificially altered genes as well as conventional insecticides actually incorporated into the organisms. These biotech modifications make the plants disease-, insect-, and/or virus-resistant in an effort to increase crop yield. Though safety research has been conducted, there's still significant concern about the health and environmental effects of GM food, which is not permitted under USDA organic standards. These foods are also referred to as GE (genetically engineered).

GROWTH HORMONES

Hormones are administered to some animals to make them gain weight and/or produce more milk. Government regulations actually prohibit the use of hormones in all poultry and pork, although poultry and pork are routinely labeled "no hormones administered." This is pure marketing. Hormones get into the meat and dairy products of conventional animals that have been treated with them. Use of hormones is banned by USDA organic standards.

INTEGRATED PEST MANAGEMENT (IPM)

An environmentally sensitive approach to preventing, identifying, and monitoring pests, IPM can be applied in agricultural settings as well as in home gardens and kitchens. Unlike organic or biodynamic farming, IPM doesn't ban the use of synthetic pesticides entirely, but relies on them only sparingly and in worst-case scenarios. For more information check out the University of California at Davis's IPM site at IPM.UCDavis.edu or the EPA's fact sheets at EPA.gov/pesticides/factsheets/ipm.htm.

IRRADIATION

The (controversial) process of exposing meat and produce to radiation to kill microorganisms, irradiation is banned by USDA organic rules.

LOCAL

Local food comes from near where you live. Different people define this differently—50 miles, 150 miles, et cetera. "Local" doesn't mean organic, nor does it always mean sustainable. Generally speaking, local farms are often ecological farms, though some certainly are not. Smaller-scale farms tend to be less likely to use chemical pesticides, fertilizers, hormones, and the like, but as there are no regulated standards for "local" food, there is no guarantee unless you know and trust your local farmer(s).

LOCAVORE

This is the widely used moniker for someone who (mainly) eats local food, also known as a "locavorian."

SUSTAINABLE AGRICULTURE

Farming that doesn't harm the environment and that does support farming communities is referred to as "sustainable." This usually also means humane worker and animal treatment. It's also referred to as "ecological" farming. There is overlap here with organic farming, but they are not always the same thing, nor is "sustainable" a regulated term.

CHAPTER ONE

what kind of food to buy

CONVENTIONAL FOOD ISN'T (FOR THE MOST PART) CONSCIOUS food. Conventional crops are sprayed with a whole host of bad-for-you and bad-for-the-earth chemical pesticides and fertilizers. It's easy as can be to avoid these sprays, keep them out of the environment, and protect farmers' health: Buy United States Department of Agriculture certified organic; the standards don't permit them. Within the world of organics, there are other choices to be made, like local versus imported or uncertified but basically organic versus certified organic. These can be confusing and time-consuming decisions. The following discussions will break down how to understand and weigh the options. Just keep in mind that whatever you wind up with in your kitchen, the most important thing you can do to protect your health and the environment, and to eat the tastiest foods, is to avoid conventional produce and products. The other debates are icing.

Packaged, processed food also isn't (for the most part) conscious food, be it conventional or organic. Stock up on whole foods whenever possible—this isn't just the name of a store. It means items as close as possible to how they sprang from the earth. Think nutrient-rich potatoes (whole) over a bag of potato chips (processed).

WHAT ORGANIC IS AND WHY TO CHOOSE IT

There are many different ways of explaining what organic is and why it's important. In the most basic terms, organic certification guarantees you non–genetically modified food that is free of chemical herbicides and pesticides, antibiotics, and hormones. All of which is proven to be better for your health and for the environment.

When it comes to fruits and vegetables, "organic" means crops raised without using most conventional pesticides, petroleum-based fertilizers, or sewage-sludge-based fertilizers. For meat, it means the animals were fed organic feed, given access to the outdoors (at least some, though critics say not enough), and never administered antibiotics or hormones. Antibiotics allow conventional farmers to overcrowd animals without risking widespread disease. They also create drug-resistant bacteria. Controversial hormones are used to promote weight gain and/or increase milk production in dairy animals. Both antibiotics and hormones can get into meat and dairy products and can affect human health.

The National Organic Standards Board's original definition of "organic" (adopted in April 1995) addresses up front that these standards allow for a gray area, that they don't mean 100 percent purity: "Organic agriculture practices cannot ensure that products are completely free of residues; however, methods are used to minimize pollution from air, soil, and water." Organics are not allowed to be genetically modified (GM), and this is crucial. GM foods aren't required to be labeled, so the public never knows when they're buying something that has been specifically manipulated to be, say, insect resistant. If you're eating conventional packaged foods, you're likely eating genetically modified soy and corn. There are potential long-term health issues and complications involved with eating GM food. The only way to know you're in the clear is to choose USDA organic.

Multiple studies have shown that organic foods may be higher in nutrients and do not contain the levels of pesticide residue that are present in their conventional counterparts. One widely quoted study published in the peer-reviewed journal *Environmental Health Perspectives* showed that children who eat organic diets have lower pesticide levels in their urine than children who eat conventional foods. The study, titled "Organic Diets Significantly Lower Children's Dietary Exposure to Organophosphorus Pesticides," was conducted by environmental and occupational health colleagues at Emory University; the University of Washington, Seattle; and the National Center for Environmental Health (part of the Centers for Disease Control and Prevention) in Atlanta. Other research has demonstrated that produce grown in nutrient-dense organic soil has higher nutrient levels than produce grown conventionally. Organic animal products also contain both higher nutrient levels and less saturated fat than their conventional counterparts, because organic animals tend to (but are not required to) be fed their natural diet (for example, grass rather than feed). They also get exercise instead of being confined to cages and pens. Still, other studies have shown the nutrient difference between organic and conventional foods aren't that great or aren't detectable. The nutrients in all foods—organic or conventional—can vary for many reasons, including where they were grown, when a fruit or vegetable was picked, how long it took to travel to your fridge, and how long it sat in your fridge before becoming dinner.

tip

Buy whole, save money: Whole foods cost less than their processed counterparts. Cutting most if not all packaged food—cookies, cereals, crackers, candy, soda, and the like—out of your grocery runs will save so much cash, all things organic (local or not) will be well within reach.

FURTHER READING ON GM

- The World Health Organization's twenty questions and answers on genetically modified foods: WHO.int/foodsafety/publications/biotech/20 questions/en
- The Sustainable Table's take: SustainableTable.org/2009/06/genetic-engineering
- Organic Consumers Association: OrganicConsumers.org
- The Institute for Responsible Technology: ResponsibleTechnology.org

Most organophiles aren't so interested in nutrient levels. They will tell you that a crucial reason to choose organic over conventional, beyond keeping pesticide residues out of their systems, is the health of the world we live in. Organic production contributes to the conservation of natural resources and keeps tons (literally) of chemical pollutants out of the soil, waterways, and air, which also protects farmers and their families. When food is produced using a chemically based system, the soil is depleted of its nutrients over time, and so more and more chemicals are needed to keep it fertile. It's up to us to ask farmers to take the best possible care of the land for future generations. Choosing organic is a simple act that makes a huge impact. And any purchase of organics affects the supply of more organics. "We want people to understand that they vote with their dollars every time they buy their food," says Jeff Moyer, farm director of the Rodale Institute, which champions organic solutions, and current chairman of the National Organic Standards Board. Voting with your dollars means that with every organic item you buy, you're letting farmers, producers, and manufacturers know you want and support organic over conventionally grown food. Farmers manage huge chunks of land, and they can manage or mismanage them based on what we as consumers ask

ORGANIC FARMING 101

Even if you don't have a green thumb, learning how organic farming works can be enlightening. Here are two great sites for more information about the regenerative nature of organic farming, how it can actually sequester atmospheric carbon, and all things relating to soil, topsoil erosion, and tilling.

- The Rodale Institute: RodaleInstitute.org
- The Leopold Center for Sustainable Agriculture: www.Leopold.IAState.edu

---

them to do. Growing organic is also important for the long-term health of our soil. Buy organic. If everyone did, we could collectively shift how food is grown overnight. "We the people have the power to change agriculture," says Moyer. "Don't buy conventional and things will change quickly."

OKAY, BUT CAN ORGANIC STANDARDS BE TRUSTED?

Yes. The system isn't perfect. Or tidy. Which is why an audit of the program was ordered in 2009, to be performed by the National Institute of Standards and Technology. But people in the know agree that the standards are trustworthy, especially with regard to domestic products. That doesn't stop others—the media, organic consumer groups, anyone with ulterior motives—from pointing out that the standards are under huge pressure from big businesses who see organics as, well, big business. Some companies want to see the standards weakened so they can grab a larger, easier, cheaper piece of the certified organic pie. The Organic Consumer Association has responded with its Millions Against Monsanto Campaign, for example. The world of organics isn't issue free. As I write, a multi-

REMIND ME AGAIN, WHY SHOULD I AVOID PESTICIDES?

The Environmental Working Group (EWG.org) puts it eloquently: "There is growing consensus in the scientific community that small doses of pesticides and other chemicals can adversely affect people, especially during vulnerable periods of fetal development and childhood, when exposures can have long-lasting effects. Because the toxic effects of pesticides are worrisome, not well understood, or in some cases, completely unstudied, shoppers are wise to minimize exposure to pesticides whenever possible."

Many of the most widely used herbicides and insecticides are banned in the European Union as well as other countries, but not in the slow-to-ban-toxic-chemicals United States. These chemicals include atrazine, one of the most used herbicides in the United States (especially on corn and sugarcane), which is a groundwater contaminant and endocrine disruptor linked to sexual abnormalities in frogs as well as increased cases of prostate cancer among the workers who produce it. Atrazine is in our drinking water and there is concern that the EPA standard for acceptable levels isn't tight enough. The chemicals also include Endosulfan, an insecticide used on fruits and vegetables as well as grains, tea, cotton, and tobacco, that lasts for years in the environment post-application. It's also an endocrine disruptor, is fatal to freshwater fish, and is in the same chemical class as the infamous DDT. I prefer my meals without, thanks. For more information on the ins and outs of these and other specific pesticides, go to the Pesticide Action Network of North America website, PANNA.org, or their eye-opening consumer-friendly site WhatsOnMyFood.org.

---

ingredient product that is only 95 percent organic can be labeled as USDA organic. This means you have to look more closely to find the things that are 100 percent organic. Milk is a particularly hot-button topic; some organic producers are purer than others. The Organic Consumer's Association (OrganicConsumers.org) and the nonprofit organic watchdog the Cornucopia Institute (Cornucopia.org) helped single out several of the largest dairies within the organic community, Horizon (Dean Foods) and Aurora Organic Dairy (the biggest private label producer), for being factory farms, even though they are certified organic. Somewhat reassuringly, the National Organic Program board responded with proposed livestock management standards changes. A version of the changes should be in effect in late 2009; at press time they still hadn't become the rule. "There are loopholes in every law. We're trying to close loopholes," says Moyer. "I think we're getting there. Our goal shouldn't be to put dairy farmers out of business but to follow a standard that is attainable but difficult to attain." Meanwhile, also in 2009, Horizon introduced nonorganic so-called natural products to the market (see page 57 for more information on this basically unregulated term), undercutting organics everywhere.

Within the organic realm, slip-ups also happen. In 2008, for example, *The Sacramento Bee* reported that a supposedly organic fertilizer used by nearly a third of California's organic farmers was actually spiked with a synthetic fertilizer that is forbidden by organic standards. Products were eventually ordered off the market, but, the article contends, a substantial portion of California's 2006 harvest of organic fruits, nuts, and vegetables wasn't technically organic.

Organic standards are not infallible. They are constantly evolving, under pressure, worth fighting for, and, for better or worse, the best thing going in terms of improving—on a large scale—how we produce food, treat our earth, and safeguard our health.

---

tip

Check price look-up (PLU) codes. These are those numbers on the pesky stickers that are impossible to get off apples. Study these to make sure you get what you think you're getting: Organic produce always begins with the number 9 and has five digits, while conventional produce begins with 4 and has four digits. Genetically modified produce starts with 8 and has five digits. GM labels are pretty rare.

WHAT LOCAL IS AND WHY TO CHOOSE IT

"Local" is much easier to define—and understand—than "certi-fied organic." It's food with low "food miles," grown near where you live, usually on small farms, and therefore doesn't travel many miles to get to your plate. Some people also refer to this as regional food. Local is what is (usually) sold at farmers' markets or at farm stands. Some people define local as being within 100 miles of your home; others push that to 250 miles or to a region of the country, such as the Midwest. However you map out your growing area (aka your foodshed), local produce is fresher than items that are shipped or flown to your grocery stores from the other side of the coun-try or the world. Often local goodies—think plums in season—are harvested just before you buy them, which also makes them more nutritious. No flavor trumps fresh picked.

Sometimes local is certified organic. Sometimes it isn't. Some-times it's sustainably grown. Sometimes it isn't. One of the benefits of buying local at farmers' markets is that it lets you directly query farmers about their growing methods. Often small local farmers are practicing some version of sustainable farming. If they use pes-ticides banned by organic standards, they tend to do so sparingly.

If we all bought our food only from big agribusiness farms, small farms would disappear. Our current large-scale farm grow-ing model mainly works because of how inexpensive (and short-sighted) it has been to ship food all over the place. But the writing is on the wall regarding cheap transportation, and the race for alternative energies is intense. Given the uncertain future of the cost of long-haul transportation, it makes sense to keep local farms alive. Some people argue they can't feed the world. It's true that my tiny local farm can't, but it feeds my family and our neighbors perfectly. And that's the point.

LOCAL VS. ORGANIC

Unless you're 100 percent organic or 100 percent local (most eco-interested eaters fall somewhere in between), it's hard to figure out how, when, and why to choose local over organic, and vice versa. Amy Topel, an educator and former food columnist for the now defunct *Green Guide*—the publication that existed before *National Geographic* bought the property—refers to this experience as "flummoxing." That's about right. "In Whole Foods they have local strawberries and organic ones," Topel says. The locals aren't organic, and the organic ones are grown halfway across the country. "I'm feeding my baby and I want him to eat organic; he should not be taking in those pesticides. For ten minutes I walked back and forth—Do I care more about my baby? Or everybody else? I ended up deciding I didn't want him to have the pesticides." This is just one instance of choosing organic over nonorganic local. This mental tug-of-war is a familiar process for those of us trying to decide what the ratio of organic to local should be in our diets, especially where kids are concerned. Pound for pound, developing little ones take in more of the harmful chemical spray residues than adults do, which is why organic is so crucial for them and for pregnant moms.

tip When you buy organic—local or otherwise—you're already purchasing a product with a drastically lower carbon footprint than its conventional counterpart, because chemical pesticides have an extremely high carbon footprint. According to Rodale's Jeff Moyer, once you eliminate the sprays, you eliminate 70 percent of the energy cost of producing a bushel of corn.

The trick to coming to peace with this local versus organic dance is to educate yourself on the concerns. If health is your main concern, then you might decide that you always want to avoid ingesting sprays that have been linked to cancer, no matter how small the amount. You'll mainly choose organic. If you decide local strawberries are the most delicious things on earth and you prefer to risk pesticide residue for a short season once a year and support small farms nearby, you're going local, especially when you can locate low-sprayed local. Soon you will arrive at your working ratio of organic to local. One suggestion: If you're feeding kids, choose domestic organic over local but lightly sprayed when buying what the Environmental Working Group refers to as "The Dirty Dozen"—the twelve most contaminated conventional fruits and vegetables (see page 45). Though if a farmer at the market says she's basically uncertified organic, and keeps pests off her strawberries using row cover (finely woven fabric placed over the crops) instead of sprays, for example, that tends to work for me.

tip

For the least expensive local organic, buy a share in a community supported agriculture farm (see page 35), shop farmers' markets at the end of the day when there may be deals, and buy in bulk when things—like tomatoes—are in full season. If you're feeling motivated, make sauce, can, or pickle them for the winter.

Bottom line: This is confusing, yes. But it's learnable and doable. It's also not a test. "Those of us concerned with this can get so caught up within the minutiae, we forget that any choice"—within the eco-arena, be it organic, local, or local and organic—"is the right choice," says Topel. "It's okay to do it halfway if at least you're doing it halfway." Amen.

MAKING THE CHOICE

One way to figure out whether to choose local or organic is to ask questions as you shop. Most people manning farmers' market

COUNTRY-OF-ORIGIN LABELS

If you do most of your shopping in a supermarket, you might have noticed that some items have country-of-origin labels (COOL). In 2009, the USDA began requiring COOL labels for "muscle cuts and ground beef (including veal), pork, lamb, goat, and chicken; wild and farm-raised fish and shellfish; fresh and frozen fruits and vegetables; peanuts, pecans, macadamia nuts, and ginseng sold by designated retailers." This system has some specific consumer-friendly benefits when it comes to fish, as certain countries are known to have highly contaminated waters and use environmentally destructive fishing methods (see chapter five). Unfortunately, COOL labels don't tell you everything about carbon footprint—miles traveled don't equal total energy cost. Still, they're a great way to know where your food is coming from, and they can help you eat closer to home. For more information: AMS.USDA.gov/cool or CountryOfOriginLabel.org.

---

stands can answer farming questions. Seek out people who are open and eager to talk, who don't get testy when you ask them about their farming practices. Even if you know nothing about agriculture or gardening, listen carefully as they explain their systems. A nonorganic farmer bringing up integrated pest management (see page 18) is a good sign. If you don't like what you hear, head to a stall selling local organic. And let any farmer you chat with know you prefer organic. Even at small markets there are always going to be big-ish farms producing food for a larger segment of the population, and they need to hear their customers clamoring for organic.

CARBON FOOTPRINT

Whenever the topic of local food and food miles comes up, inevitably so does the issue of carbon footprint. Yes, food can rack

·THE LIST: WHAT TO BUY

A sliding scale of choices from best to worst

- Local organic from CSA farms and farmers' markets
- Local sustainably grown or raised, no spray
- Certified organic, domestic
- Local low spray/integrated pest management only
- Certified organic, international, country-of-origin information a must

AVOID: Conventional, sprayed

up a serious footprint, and some items are especially bad offenders (conventional beef comes to mind). There's something compelling and tidy about the notion of being able to stamp something as "low carbon"—which some companies (notably UK-based Tesco) and countries (notably Sweden) are trying to do—but I'm not convinced that calculating the complete greenhouse gas emissions caused by growing and transporting an apple, a hunk of parmesan, or a bottle of beer is possible, or even the right way to think about food. The math involved can get pretty convoluted. Can you really factor in every last detail, from the footprints of the conventional petrochemical sprays, to labor, to packaging, and to transportation? And what about how far laborers themselves drove to get to a farm? While the formal assessments (aka life-cycle assessments (LCAs); see page 161) used to calculate carbon footprints are confusing, they're worth considering—especially with regard to which country to buy wine from based on where you live or things like plastic sandwich bags versus wax paper bags. But they shouldn't be the only thing considered when deciding what to eat.

SOME RESOURCES

CARBON FOOTPRINT

Sites

Carbon Trust: an organization that helps others reduce carbon emissions and is involved with developing new low-carbon technologies. CarbonTrust.co.uk

The Carbon Neutral Company: a carbon-offset and management business. CarbonNeutral.com

Carbon Trade Watch: a social justice group. CarbonTradeWatch.org

Food Climate Research Network: a research group focused on reducing global greenhouse-gas impacts of UK food consumption. FCRN.org.uk

Books and Reports

Carbon Counter by Mark Lynas

The Food and Farming Transition: Toward a Post Carbon Food System by Richard Heinberg and Michael Bomford. Download this report at PostCarbon.org/food.

ORGANICS AND LOCAL FOOD

The Omnivore's Dilemma and *In Defense of Food* by Michael Pollan

Organic, Inc.: Natural Foods and How They Grew by Samuel Fromartz

Coming Home to Eat: The Pleasures and Politics of Local Foods by Gary Paul Nabhan

fruits, vegetables, and where to shop

TRADITIONAL GROCERY STORES DON'T TEND TO BE THE greatest place to shop for local or organic foods, as they generally don't carry a wide variety of these items. Better alternatives include farmers' markets and stands selling local produce (double-check—the stand closest to me is filled with fruit that comes from across the country), buying a share in a farm via community supported agriculture, and planting your own vegetables. If supermarkets are your only option—as is the case for many of us—there are ways to approach them to find the most sustainable items they offer. This includes keeping an eye out for COOL labels, even if the items are organic—in-season produce should be as local as possible. Midsummer tomatoes from as far away as Chile aren't the best option. This also includes knowing what to buy when organic isn't available, and what to do about exotic supermarket produce, like bananas, that may not grow anywhere near you but have become everyday staples.

SUPERMARKETS

You can find "green" food in most every supermarket, if you know how to navigate. This involves sticking to the outskirts of the store—fruits, veggies, milk, eggs, cheese, freshly baked bread, and meat all tend to be on the periphery of most supermarkets. In the middle is a vast sea of packaged goods. To make the best food choices, steer clear of the middle. In certain chains, the organic and so-called natural items are lumped together in a separate area. Look for items with the USDA organic stamp and for other meaningful certifications. Read ingredient lists obsessively. Ask the super-market management if anything is local and see if they'd be willing to stock items you want but don't see. By being savvy, you'll come out with (reusable) bags full of the best items any store has to offer.

FARMERS' MARKETS

If you can figure out how to do all of your shopping at farmers' markets, go for it. That's the idea. Sometimes, though, it's easier said than done. Northeastern locavores may envy Californians and their year-round ample markets, but if you have any farmers' markets in your area, count your blessings. There are some places in the country where there are none. If you don't have access to one, try to join or create a co-op or a buyers' club (see an example at FarmBuyersClub.com) or at least locate a few farmers near you via LocalHarvest.org. And absolutely cozy up to your supermarket's manager so you can get her to carry what you want. "Any grocer worth their salt is going to be responsive," says Dan Barber, executive chef and co-owner of Blue Hill at Stone Barns and a board member of the Stone Barns Center for Food and Agriculture in Pocantico

Hills, New York. "The major chains are really responsive, even people who have been asleep for so long. If there are six comment cards that are the same theme, it automatically comes to the table of the board meeting. These businesses have such small margins of profit that they'll do anything that's going to win over customers."

COMMUNITY SUPPORTED AGRICULTURE (CSA)

Here's how my CSA farmer, Deb Kavakos of Stoneledge Farm, defines this system on her website (StoneledgeFarmNY.org): "Community Supported Agriculture is a relationship of mutual support and commitment between local farmers and community members. CSA membership is a partnership with the farm, sharing both the bounty of the farm's harvest and some of the risks involved with regional production. In return for an annual membership fee to cover the costs of production of the farm, members receive a weekly share of the freshest, highest quality, organic produce during the farm's growing season. CSA members are directly supporting regional small family farms while receiving the freshest organic produce."

My family has been a member of Deb's farm for a decade. It brings us more than wonderful food; it brings us hope in what seems to be an increasingly polluted, toxic world. People like to provoke me by telling me that local agriculture isn't and cannot be the way of the future. I think the naysayers would change their minds if they

tip

To locate nearby farmers' markets or to join a CSA, go online. Try JustFood.org for New York City or WAFarmers Markets.com for Washington State. For national search engines, check out the USDA websites: NAL .USDA.gov/afsic/csa and APPS.AMS.USDA .gov/FarmersMarkets; LocalHarvest.org; LocallyGrown.net/ Markets/List; Kerr Center.com; and FarmersMarket.com.

could have seen the difference in the farm between my first visit in 2000 and my most recent in 2008. Stoneledge has grown a tremendous amount and appears to have turned into a viable, sustainable business for Deb's whole family. It's feeding more and more people and has already kept untold thousands of pounds of industrial chemicals out of the earth.

CSA is also the least expensive way to buy organic produce. What we get per week during growing season would cost significantly more if purchased at a farmers' market. Through my CSA, I can also get honey, syrup, fruit, coffee, bread, and flowers. I've even been connected to a separate pastured meat and poultry CSA. It's a wonderful network to be part of.

That said, CSA isn't for everyone. Some people prefer to choose their own vegetables, rather than take what is allotted to them of what happened to grow that week. Or they're out of town too much. Others—like Joan Gussow, author of *This Organic Life: Confessions of a Suburban Homesteader*, nutritionist, and Columbia professor emeritus—enjoy growing their own food and worry that CSA farming removes the consumer too much from the act of growing. A former member of the National Organic Standards Board, Gussow thinks the lesson that food doesn't grow automatically is invaluable. I find that lesson is learned more by CSA members than farmers' market shoppers, and certainly more than supermarket shoppers, because we share the risks involved with farming.

tip

Got kids? Bring them to help pick up your CSA share, or take them when food shopping in general. Having a personal connection to the vegetables often results in more vegetables eaten.

During a nasty Northeastern tomato and potato blight in 2009, for example, local non-CSA farmers were going into debt because they lost their crops, but CSA farmers were okay; members shared the sad loss. And their farms were planted with many other diverse vegetables. Sometimes my greens

EMERIL LAGASSE'S QUICK BRAISED GREENS

Chef Emeril Lagasse may not be as well known for his show on Planet Green as he is for his many moons spent on Food Network, but he's the biggest named chef on Discovery's sustainable living network. He tackles greens—any seasonal versions a farmer might sell—by quick-braising them, a technique that uses very little cooking energy. A perfect side dish.

Serves 2 to 4

2 tablespoons olive oil

1/2 teaspoon crushed red pepper flakes

1 1/2 tablespoons thinly sliced garlic

2 bunches lacinata kale, Swiss chard, or collard greens, cut into 1-inch pieces

1 cup vegetable broth or water

1 teaspoon salt

1/4 teaspoon cayenne pepper

In a large skillet over medium heat, heat the olive oil. After 10 to 15 seconds, add the crushed red pepper and garlic, and cook until fragrant, 30 to 45 seconds. Add the greens in batches, stirring between additions until the greens wilt slightly. Cook, stirring, for 2 minutes. Add the broth, salt, and cayenne. Cover and continue to cook until the greens are just tender, 4 to 5 minutes longer.

THE LIST: WHERE TO SHOP
A sliding scale of choices from best to worst

- Farmers' markets, farm stands selling local food, and CSA farms
- Natural food markets and "health food" stores; bigger natural food chains like Whole Foods; specialty online retailers; small shops that specialize in one thing (i.e., a produce store, a cheese store, a butcher shop), where you know the people and can ask questions

AVOID IF POSSIBLE: national supermarket chains without any organic options, convenience stores stocked with packaged foods

have little holes in them where a bug got to them before me—perfectly fine to eat, just not the most gorgeous things to look at, so they wouldn't sell well in a market setting. Or some years we get very few eggplants, or cucumbers, or peppers, or whatever isn't growing well that year. That connects farm share members to the weather and the land in a unique way. It's not just a bag of goods to be picked up every week; it can be an education.

A SUPERMARKET-FREE LIFE: ONE EXTREME CASE

If being able to avoid supermarkets altogether is a concept that appeals to you, hearing how other people manage to do it can be inspirational. I'm not entirely store-free (yet) myself, but I have enough access to farmers' market and CSA produce, and alternative sources for pure dairy and meat, that I have replaced my supermarket runs with infrequent jaunts to a health food store for staples, mainly during colder months. It feels good. But, like most Americans, I'm reliant on others for my food, especially since I don't have a yard or a terrace to grow my own. Joan Gussow is one

JOAN GUSSOW'S ROASTED WHAT'S-IN-THE-GARDEN

This isn't really a recipe—which makes it the perfect recipe. It's seasonal and doesn't call for anything that isn't growing in the same region (Gussow's yard!) at the same time. Plus it gives wonderful insight into the mind-set of a deeply green thinker. "I tend to make things that are related to what I have. I save recipes when they come along, but I don't make as much use of cookbooks as I might. They have an assortment of things I might not have. If I were thinking about dinner during the day, I am thinking of the fridge: What's in it should I use up? What's in the garden I should use up? I'm aware of what I have at a given time. I had my first Burbank russets this year that were big. I love to dig potatoes. It's a pleasure, like finding gold in the earth—a wonderful bucketful of potatoes comes out of the ground. I rolled them in oil and stuck them in the hot oven. Then I thought, I'm not going to waste that oven heat." She remembered that a friend had done a potato-and-green-beans thing, and called her to find out how to proceed. She wound up roasting potatoes, green beans, and Jimmy Nardello peppers on separate sheets in the oven for about a half hour. "It wasn't a meal," she says. "It was potatoes and green beans and peppers on a plate. And it was delicious."

of the completely store-free. In her Northeastern garden, Gussow grows everything from artichokes to figs, and has raspberries that put out "fiercely" until November. She grows so much that she doesn't even go to the farmers' market. The only fruit she purchases in the winter is a box of mail order grapefruit. It's a treat, as she believes people who don't live near where fruit grows year-round aren't meant to have it in the winter. She relies on nature and makes do with what she has.

WANT A HOME GARDEN?

Home and urban rooftop gardens have really bolted in popularity of late. There was a victory garden planted in front of San Francisco City Hall for Slow Food Nation in 2008 (SlowFoodUSA.org). Then, in 2009, First Lady Michelle Obama had one planted on the White House lawn, and Agriculture Secretary Tom Vilsack turned a stretch of pavement in front of the USDA's national headquarters into a People's Garden. Growing your own veggies has become so hip that people with more money on their hands than time are even paying other people to put gardens in their yards for them. It's pretty hard to ever pay four dollars a pound for organic summer squash when you see what your own plant will yield.

There are many ways to grow your own—from window boxes to a full-fledged garden. Whatever you're planting in, make sure to test your soil for contaminants you don't want in your food. If you're using raised beds or are growing food in boxes, double-check with your garden center if the wood or containers are safe for edible plants. This is one instance where recycling a container—or, say, a rubber tire, which can contain lead, a neurotoxin, plus benzene and phthalates, among other undesirables—as a planter isn't a good idea. And don't forget to use organic soil.

MY FRUITS AND VEGGIES: A 365-DAY OVERVIEW

Sometimes, even after reading about what to shop for and where to shop, it's still hard to figure out how to make it work in day-to-day life. Here's an inside look at how I determine the organic to local ratio on my table, and where I snag my fruits and veggies from. It's an ever-evolving process, based on what's currently available. Each year we go greener. I live in New York City, which means that there are certain times of the year when an exclusively local diet means mainly eating stored root vegetables, unless I have canned, preserved, and frozen produce earlier in the year. Ninety-nine percent of the time, despite my best intentions, I have not. While at this point in life I'm willing to eat mainly roots, the other eaters in my home are not. We're lucky to have year-round farmers' markets, some with greenhouse-grown greens, but the best one is a subway ride or long wintry walk away from our apartment, which is especially hard with a preschooler in tow. This is our basic guideline for what produce we eat throughout the year at home.

Vegetables

June through Thanksgiving, our vegetables come from our local, certified organic CSA farm. We supplement our weekly pickups, especially in tomato and corn season, at farmers' markets.

From Thanksgiving to June, we buy a mix of local/organic and local/sustainable—whatever is still being sold at our farmers' markets—as well as some domestic USDA organic items bought at a health food store. As deepest winter sets in, this ratio can tip in favor of the store-bought items, though each year I get closer to being more local than not. The moment the outdoor markets show new life again, usually around March, we're back at them exclusively until our CSA restarts. We try not to be too dogmatic.

Fruit

July through Thanksgiving, most of our fruit comes via a share offered by our CSA farmer. It's regional, not certified organic, from low-spray orchards dedicated to integrated pest management and chosen by my CSA farmer, whom I obviously trust. We also supplement from farmers' markets.

LOCAL FOODS PRIMERS

If you don't know exactly what's in season and when in your region, get help from a Local Foods Wheel, which you can find at LocalFoodsWheel.com. At the time of publication, they were available only for the San Francisco Bay and New York metro areas, but wheels for more regions are likely in the works. Another wheel for the New York area can be found at ChewOnThis.org. If you have an iPhone or an iPod Touch, you can download the application "Locavore" to track what's in season near you (as well as find places to buy it). If none of these applies to you, do a little Googling to find out what's growing—and when—near you.

After Thanksgiving, we keep right on buying pears and apples from farmers' markets. Come winter, fruit is my weakness, and its food mile–heavy carbon footprint weighs on my mind. I always ask for citrus as a holiday present. Nothing makes me happier than the arrival of a box of organic pixie tangerines—usually from California or Texas. In my freezer are stored no-spray strawberries from a favorite local farmer and wild Canadian blueberries. I froze the former, the latter are a packaged splurge from our health food store (my daughter adores them). Most of the fresh fruit at my health food store is from New Zealand come winter. I avoid this.

WINTER OPTIONS FOR LOCAVORES

Enough people are trying to figure out how to eat as locally as possible during the winter months in cold climates that some excellent new options are popping up. Take Winter Sun Farms, for example (WinterSunFarms.com). They partner with local sustainable farms, buying and freezing surplus crops during the growing season, then offering a frozen CSA share of sorts come winter. A very cool business model. I've read of similar CSAs that offer canned or preserved products. There are also a number of winter farmers' markets across the country, some indoors, some outdoors, selling a mix of cellared root vegetables, canned goods, frozen pastured meat, cheese, and greenhouse greens. These tend to happen only once a month. With growing interest in sustainable agriculture, and a burgeoning locavore movement, the number of such outlets will continue to increase. It almost makes the first frost bearable. Still, it's hard not to be jealous of Hawaiians. Imagine how easy it would be to maintain a local winter diet if you had organic exotic fruit growing nearby.

A FRUITY SITUATION

Sourcing conundrums can be a headache. In the Northeast, for example, it's difficult to locate local certified organic fruit, which is why my CSA fruit share isn't organic even though my veggies are. When my daughter was old enough to appreciate going apple picking for the first time, I didn't want her on an orchard that had been sprayed. After much searching, I found a few safe places to

---

THE LIST: IF YOU CAN'T FIND ORGANIC
A sliding scale of choices from best to worst

- Substitute a similar ingredient that is organic
- Choose a local version you know to be low sprayed
- Choose a conventional version if it is on the Environmental Working Group's Clean Fifteen (least sprayed) list (see page 45)

AVOID: Any conventional fruit or vegetable on the Environmental Working Group's Dirty Dozen list

go. "Fruit in this part of the country is one of the more difficult things to grow organically," explains the Rodale Institute's farm director, Jeff Moyer. "People like fruit and so do insects. In this humid climate we have a lot of diseases to account for. We can do that through variety selection, but some varieties aren't the ones people are accustomed to buying in the supermarket."

It's ironic that the well-known varieties are the ones most susceptible to disease, and therefore need to be sprayed. Farmers aren't likely to grow unfamiliar varieties that don't require spraying (or as much spraying) in the hopes that consumers will buy them because, unlike annual vegetables, apple trees are something a farmer will plant and harvest for twenty years. If they guess wrong, as to consumer taste or buying habits, they're in serious trouble. That said, there are some orchards managing to produce all-organic apples. The next time you're going apple picking in the Northeast, head to Rodale's own farm in Pennsylvania (Rodale Institute.org) if you can make the trek. They have 1,100 organic "U-pick" trees. If you find an organic orchard online, make sure you get someone on the phone before showing up to pick. In the Hudson Valley, Prospect Hill Orchards in Milton, New York (ProspectHillOrchards.com), for example, cleared new land and planted five acres of organic orchards in 2004 and are one of the few certified organic fruit growers in New York. Well worth supporting, but their U-pick is IPM-only, not the organic goodies.

tip To find organic orchards in other parts of the country, look them up on Local Harvest.org or PickYourOwn.org.

THE EXOTICS CONUNDRUM

There are a number of items in your fruit bowl (and in your cabinets—see chapter seven) that might be certified organic but

THE DIRTY DOZEN AND THE CLEAN FIFTEEN

The Environmental Working Group (EWG) ranks pesticide contamination for forty-seven popular fruits and vegetables to let consumers know what items they should absolutely buy organic, and which conventional ones are the least contaminated. To see the full results, learn more about their methodology, or see updated lists, check out FoodNews.org. Download the list and stick it in your wallet so you'll always have it with you to consult while shopping. The EWG says consumers can lower their pesticide exposure by almost 80 percent by avoiding the top twelve most contaminated fruits and vegetables and eating the fifteen least contaminated instead. They based their rankings on nearly 87,000 tests for pesticides on produce collected by the USDA and the FDA between 2000 and 2007. Here are their results, listed in order:

THE DIRTY DOZEN: BUY THESE ORGANIC

1 Peach	5 Nectarine	9 Lettuce
2 Apple	6 Strawberries	10 Grapes (imported)
3 Bell Pepper	7 Cherries	11 Carrot
4 Celery	8 Kale	12 Pear

THE CLEAN FIFTEEN: LOWEST IN PESTICIDES

1 Onion	6 Asparagus	11 Papaya
2 Avocado	7 Sweet Peas	12 Watermelon
3 Sweet Corn	8 Kiwi	13 Broccoli
4 Pineapple	9 Cabbage	14 Tomato
5 Mango	10 Eggplant	15 Sweet Potato

fall into the realm of still not being great to buy. In this realm, no exotic is more widely available, or controversial, than the banana.

The ubiquitous yellow fruit is nature's perfect answer to packaged goods—every parent's nutrient-dense dream snack. Yet, it's a deeply flawed food. It's pretty much the poster fruit for how confusing trying to eat consciously can be. Bananas are grown very far away, are environmentally destructive, are often harvested under conditions unfair to laborers, and the variety we all eat will apparently be extinct in the not-so-distant future. The greenest and most environmentally devoted eaters around don't eat bananas, or refer to them as a guilty pleasure.

Depending on where you live, if you think about where bananas actually come from, it's shocking how inexpensive they are. The price alone should make you wonder how much the people working the trees are being paid. As Dan Koeppel, author of *Banana: The Fate of the Fruit That Changed the World*, wrote in *The New York Times:* "That bananas have long been the cheapest fruit at the grocery store is astonishing. They're grown thousands of miles away, they must be transported in cooled containers and even then they survive no more than two weeks after they're cut off the tree." Koeppel contrasts this with far pricier apples, some of which are grown close to the stores they're sold in and keep for months. Americans eat as many bananas as apples and oranges combined. Food for thought.

Choosing to eat these long-haul snacks may soon not even be an option. Koeppel explains that the Cavendish variety of banana that all importers currently sell (used in part because all Cavendishes in a given shipment will ripen at the same time) comes from the same gene pool. Experts estimate that a fungus that is virulent enough to wipe out these banana trees will reach Latin America anytime between five and twenty years from now. It sounds impossible, but there's historical precedent. Our direct ancestors ate

tip

There is a local alternative to the banana. The cookbook author and chef Deborah Madison suggests pawpaws, the American fruit (aka native persimmons) indigenous to twenty-six states. They're available on the East Coast in September, and originally grew only as far west as Nebraska, but are now grown even in California. If you've never seen them in your markets, you can order them online (for a pretty penny) from HeritageFoodsUSA.com.

another variety, the Gros Michel, which was wiped out by a fungus taking down entire plantations in the 1950s. The loss of the Cavendish will be sad for those of us who like to eat them, but we'll survive. It won't be as simple for the farmers who grow them, who rely on that income and don't have the means to diversify. If you're eating bananas, the farmers are another reason to buy only fair trade (see page 106), not to mention organic.

BEYOND BANANAS: OTHER EXOTICS

Kiwi, mango, papaya, pineapple, and the like are all also readily available and can be found stamped "organic." Even if you can find them only conventionally grown, many of them score well on the Clean Fifteen list. They're pricier than bananas, but they're just as exotic for most Americans. Still, in the dead of cold-and-flu winter, it's hard not to think about how kiwis have even higher levels of vitamin C than the citrus that may also grow nowhere near you. If you're going to eat them, check the COOL label—they're usually from far-away New Zealand, but sometimes they're from California. Definitely opt for domestic in season when possible. Keep in mind that imported exotics rarely taste very good. Think about it— when was the last time you actually had a good mango in Utah or Michigan or South Dakota in January? They're usually hard and grim, and not worth the cash or the environmental impact.

tip

Washing and peeling produce doesn't get rid of pesticides. It may reduce some spray residue, but it won't eliminate it entirely, since the sprays get inside the fruits and vegetables as they grow. In fact, the EWG lists (see page 45) are mainly based on rinsed and peeled produce. And remember that peeling also removes nutrients.

CHAPTER THREE

farm animals

LET'S GET THIS OUT OF THE WAY: BEING A VEGETARIAN OR A vegan might be the single best thing you can do for the environment. Not to mention, obviously, for animals. It's well documented that the conventional factory-farm method of raising animals for food—especially cattle—is an energy-intensive, inhumane (for animals and workers), water-guzzling, poisonous-emissions-releasing, earth-polluting endeavor. Most of us who want to be vegetarians already are. I, for the record, am not. Omnivores who have no interest in giving up their bacon or steaks should switch to sustainable, humane versions of their favorite proteins. Immediately. Another way to reduce environmental impact: Eat less meat. Drop the number of times a week you eat meat, decrease the ounces per serving, think of it as a side dish, or do all of the above to instantly reduce its environmental burden. Swap in some chicken when you would eat beef; poultry treads lighter than cattle. Bonus: Eating less meat costs less. Spend the extra cash on better meat.

The following pages are devoted to explaining what sustainable meat is, and how and where to find it. I cannot overstate how substantially this small personal shift can bring about large-scale change for the better. Car/meat metaphors have been used in several often-quoted diet and climate change reports over the past few years; hamburgers have even been referred to as "Hummers on a plate." Environmentalists say that if all Americans suddenly started buying only grass-fed beef, our environmental issues would be over. This is an exaggeration, and at present there isn't enough to go around anyway, but there's more than a kernel of truth here. I'll touch on the impact of industrial-scale meat manufacturing some in this chapter, but this topic has been covered effectively and in depth by other writers, filmmakers, and organizations (see sidebar, pages 50–51). Since reading their accounts and doing my own research, I do not *ever* eat conventionally raised and produced meat. I suggest you don't either. Another reason to minimize your intake: The very pesticide residues you attempt to avoid by eating ecologically farmed produce actually accumulate in meat, making it more toxic than plant-based food.

LABELS, LABELS EVERYWHERE

When out shopping for meat, would that there were only two options: conventional or organic. That would make a concerned consumer's choice uncomplicated and clear. The reality is that there are numerous labels and very few watchdog groups monitoring their application. If meat isn't organic—a government-regulated term—there's really almost nothing a farmer or a manufacturer can't say about their product. The number of monikers is astounding. It's difficult to know, standing in front of mound after mound of ground meat at the store and under pressure to get dinner on the table, what these claims actually mean, and who—if anyone—is regulating them. The more you shop for "good" meat, the more familiar you will become with the terms and you will be better able to understand which are actually trustworthy. As with all food, there's a leap of faith to be made here when not buying certified organic, which remains the most trustworthy and regulated label you'll find on meat. For people interested primarily in animal welfare as their reason for buying conscious meat, the organic standards may not go far enough.

A LABELS PRIMER

Here's the essential breakdown of meat certifications and claims, ordered by how trustworthy they are, with the best at the top. The labeling information is largely from ConsumerReports.org Greener Choices Eco Labels (bookmark it now: GreenerChoices.org/eco-labels). Keep in mind that these labels and the regulations they stand for can—and do—change from time to time. For the most up-to-date versions, plus new shields and stamps, I must defer to the speed of the Internet. Check the site occasionally to stay current.

A MEAT EDUCATION

There's nothing like seeing to make you believe and hasten your switch from factory-farmed animals. Check out these films for (graphic) depictions of slaughter; debeaked, unnaturally big-breasted, and over-crowded chickens; waste-strewn feedlots with acres of crammed cattle, some barely standing; and horribly mistreated workers. If you can't stomach the images, you're better off reading the following books and websites—a small selection of what's out there on the topic.

SEE

- *Food, Inc.* (FoodIncMovie.com)
- *Fast Food Nation* (FoxSearchlight.com/fastfoodnation)
- *The Meatrix* (These award-winning factory-farming videos from Sustainable Table are animated, so are slightly easier to take—see TheMeatrix.com)

SURF

- The Humane Society of the United States: HumaneSociety.org/issues/campaigns/factory_farming

USDA ORGANIC

"USDA Organic" (AMS.USDA.gov/NOP) is a third-party-certified, government-regulated claim signifying that the animal never ate any animal by-products (which have been directly linked to transmission of mad cow disease, and are often fed to natural vegetarians); was never administered antibiotics or hormones; had access to fresh air, sunlight, and had freedom of movement; and ruminants (cows and sheep) had access to pasture/grass. Also, it ate organic feed, grown without pesticides and artificial fertilizers. Someone claiming to adhere to "organic practices" may be doing so, but this is not a regulated claim. Look for the stamp.

CERTIFIED HUMANE

"Certified Humane Raised and Handled" (CertifiedHumane.org) is a meaningful label that indicates that meat, dairy, and egg products came from animals that were treated humanely. Growth

- The Organic Consumers Association: OrganicConsumers.org/toxic/factoryfarm.cfm
- Natural Resources Defense Council: NRDC.org/water/pollution/farms.asp
- Sustainable Table: SustainableTable.org
- Chefs Collaborative: ChefsCollaborative.org
- Farm Sanctuary: FarmSanctuary.org/issues/factoryfarming
- FactoryFarm.org

READ
- *Fast Food Nation* by Eric Schlosser
- *What to Eat* by Marion Nestle
- *Salad Bar Beef* by Joel Salatin, farmer (PolyFaceFarms.com)
- *Real Food* by Nina Planck
- *Deeply Rooted: Unconventional Farmers in the Age of Agribusiness* by Lisa M. Hamilton

tip

If you're worried about mad cow disease, both USDA certified organic and biodynamic standards do not permit cattle to be fed animal by-products including the blood, organ parts, and nerve tissue that are the chief means of transmitting this brain-wasting illness. Eating grass-fed cattle, bred on the farm you trust, that never eat feed renders the danger virtually nonexistent.

hormones are prohibited, as are antibiotics in the feed. However, antibiotics can be used in the treatment of sick animals. From birth through slaughter, animals must have access to clean and sufficient food and water as well as have a safe and healthful living environment. Producers must also comply with specific environmental standards. Processors must comply with the American Meat Institute Standards, a more strict set of guidelines for slaughtering farm animals than required by the Federal Humane Slaughter Act. All Certified Humane standards were developed by a team of animal scientists and veterinarians, and are based in part on the UK's Royal Society for the Prevention of Cruelty to Animals' standards.

GRASS-FED

"Grass-fed" refers to cows and other ruminants (animals that chew cud, like sheep) that are permitted to eat grass, which they're naturally supposed to eat, and do not require other resource-intensive food (such as soy). USDA verification for the claim is voluntary, and the term "grass-fed" is unregulated. Only beef and lamb carrying the "USDA Process Verified" shield, along with the claim "U.S. Grass-Fed," have actually chosen to be verified. "Grass-fed"

ODD BUT TRUE

Haylage, says Jessica Applestone of Fleisher's Grass-fed and Organic Meats, is "slightly frizzante, alcoholic," so cows love it.

A FEW EXTRA WORDS ON GRASS-FED BEEF

Some grass-fed steers are finished with grain. Even organic standards permit it. "Finishing" refers to the few months cattle are fattened up before slaughter. Many people prefer the taste of grain-finished beef; it's familiar, since most American cattle are grain-fed, which produces fattier, blander meat that is easier to cook than its grass-fed counterpart. It's juicier, more forgiving. Corn- and grain-fed cattle grow faster, often with the help of hormones, protein supplements, and antibiotics, and are more profitable, since you can slaughter them younger. The purest stuff out there is grass-fed and grass finished. Grain finishing decreases nutrients. Truly 100 percent grass-fed beef is very low in fat and is a rare and seasonal product. If someone is selling fresh (unfrozen) 100 percent grass-fed meat when there isn't grass on the ground, it can't be the real deal. During these months, grass-fed cattle can eat silage and haylage (those big round balls you see in fields covered in plastic), but they don't gain weight. Farmers won't slaughter an animal that isn't actively gaining weight and will hold off until they're back on living grass. Ask questions or read the fine print to find truly grass-fed products. Also look for the word "pastured." It's one thing to be fed some grass in confinement, and another to eat it out in the open pasture. Organic ruminants aren't required to be pastured, though most are.

means that animals were raised on a lifetime diet of 100 percent grass and forage (with the exception of milk consumed prior to weaning), including legumes and cereal grain crops. Animals must have access to pasture during most of the growing season, and cannot be fed grain or grain products, which can diminish the nutritive benefits of grass feeding. The standard does not exclude the use of antibiotics and hormones (these are covered under separate standards). Keep in mind that grass-fed standards are for ruminant animal meat only, so the claim on pork or poultry doesn't mean anything. For information on grass-fed dairy products, see page 69.

ENVIRONMENTAL BENEFITS OF GRASS-FEEDING ANIMALS

- Grass-fed animals bring up over-grazing concerns like soil erosion and water quality issues, but well-managed grass-fed animals rotate pastures, which allows for regrowth.

- Manure, when not concentrated in a feedlot, fertilizes soil naturally instead of becoming hazardous waste.

- Healthy grass can absorb carbon and help offset fossil-fuel emissions.

- Pasture is not a petroleum-intensive crop. Farmers don't need synthetic pesticides or fertilizers to grow it.

- Pastured meat tends to be local meat, which decreases food miles.

- Grass-fed animals are healthier than feedlot grain-fed animals and are less likely to require antibiotics.

FREE RANGE/FREE ROAMING

This is not a very meaningful or verified claim. The USDA has defined "free range" or "free roaming" for poultry products only, and this doesn't actually include eggs—meaning you can buy free-range chicken and have some idea of what that means for the animal when it was alive, but the claim isn't meant to be applied to eggs. For other products—or animals—carrying the "free range" label, there is no standard definition or regulation. The USDA requires that birds have been given access to the outdoors, but considers as little as five minutes of open-air access each day to be adequate. Most "free range" chickens do have access to a small outdoor pen, but they may not ever visit it. Keep in mind that "free range" doesn't have any bearing on feed or indicate that the bird was raised on a nonfactory farm. Inspections are said to be few and far between. Interesting fact: The

tip

Get your info to go: Download the wallet-sized Glossary of Meat Production Methods from Sustainable Table's website: SustainableTable.org. Go print it now.

WATER AND METHANE

Raising cattle requires an obscene amount of water (a dairy cow drinks 25 to 50 gallons daily, according to the USDA), and they produce an outrageous amount of methane (a greenhouse gas). Some people wonder how this matters—the cows would be here on earth anyway, right? Wrong. Livestock aren't the same thing as wild animals. The billions of them we humans breed for food could never be sustained on the planet in the wild and so aren't considered part of the natural carbon cycle. So, even though it comes from animals, livestock methane is actually man-made. I've read reports stating that grass-fed animals actually produce more methane than grain-fed, and still others saying the opposite. The best thing for anyone to do is eat less meat across the board.

---

highly meaningful organic label on poultry products doesn't define this free-range issue, either.

FRESH

This is a USDA-regulated claim for poultry only, indicating that a raw poultry product has not been cooled below 26°F. It's not a meaningful claim, and is potentially deceptive, as "fresh" is generally used to mean something that hasn't been frozen, processed, or preserved. But do the math: Twenty-six degrees is actually eight degrees below freezing.

NO HORMONES ADMINISTERED

Hormones are an issue only when it comes to ruminants, as the USDA prohibits their use in raising hogs and poultry. So, the claim on pork and poultry products is redundant and mainly a sales gimmick. Hormones are used to promote growth and stimulate muscle development. Though the term "hormone free" is sometimes used, it is actually considered "unapprovable" by the USDA on any meat products (my hunch is this is political). Producers are allowed to label their products "no hormones administered." This unverified claim implies that the animal must not have received any added hormones during the course of its lifetime. See the claim on beef or lamb and you can assume it's probably free of any added hormones and that the manufacturer has gone beyond USDA regulations for conventional meat production.

ANTIBIOTIC-FREE

Like "hormone free," this designation is considered "unapprovable" by the USDA on any meat products, so producers instead label meat and poultry with the claim "no antibiotics administered" or "raised without antibiotics." There is no verification system in place, but if the USDA happens to catch a company lying, they won't let them use the claim. At many factory farms, anti-

---

EVEN MINIMALLY REGULATED CLAIMS CAN HELP

The USDA certainly doesn't regulate claims like "free range" or "no hormones or antibiotics administered" as well as it does "USDA organic." But it does actually slap producers on the wrist—by fining them or revoking their claim—for stating things that aren't true. For example, in 2008, they rescinded the "raised without antibiotics" label from Tyson Chicken. (According to Marion Nestle in her tome *What to Eat*, Tyson Foods controls about 25 percent of the entire United States market for chicken, beef, and pork). The ruling came as little surprise to their competition—or to savvy consumers—as the price per pound was too low to actually have been raised the right way. In fact, Sanderson Farms and Perdue Farms were the ones who alerted the USDA to the misuse of the label.

According to one chicken producer, in the aftermath of the rescinding, the USDA required everyone claiming to be raising without antibiotics to give affidavits swearing they were being honest. So Tyson's misuse of the claim actually strengthened it. "It's a federal offense," says Murray's Chicken owner Steve Gold (MurraysChicken.com). "You don't want to screw around—either you're real or you're not real."

POULTRY FEED

According to the nonprofit organization Sustainable Table, pastured poultry might be eating grasses, worms, and bugs plus supplementary feed like corn, oats, soybeans, and dried alfalfa. A factory-farmed conventional chicken may be eating meat and bone meal from post-slaughter animal waste, antibiotics, and even arsenic! Yes, arsenic, which can cause a variety of health problems in humans, including poisoning, cancer, sore throats, and warts. It can also interfere with thyroid function. Used to promote chicken growth, add pigment to flesh, and prevent disease, it gets into the meat, the feces (which are sometimes fed to conventional cattle), and eventually the water supply near the farm. To avoid ingesting arsenic or contributing to the problem, choose organic, or speak to your sustainable farmer about which chicken feed they use before buying.

biotics are used to prevent diseases caused by crowding and unnatural diets. The overuse of antibiotics can lead to bacterial resistance that threatens human health. One Johns Hopkins study says workers in poultry factories are thirty-two times more likely to be infected with antibiotic-resistant *E. coli* than people who work in other trades.

NATURAL

This claim has been used by manufacturers for a long time on meat to signify it is minimally processed and free of artificial additives, including dyes, flavorings, and chemical preservatives. At publication time, the USDA's Food Safety and Inspection Service was in the middle of reassessing the "natural" claim and how best to coordinate it with the Agricultural Marketing Service's definition of "naturally raised," which prohibits growth promoters, antibiotics, and animal or fish by-products in feed. Either way, it's a voluntary standard, not a third-party-certified one. The term certainly implies a great deal, and at best it means safer-than-conventional practices. "Natural" doesn't actually pertain to anything with regard to humane treatment, access to pasture, or what kind of farm the animals were raised on. Buyer beware.

WHERE TO SHOP

Now that you know what labels to look for, it's time to reconsider where you shop. Supermarkets often stock only conventionally raised meat; those shrink-wrapped identical cuts sitting on toxic Styrofoam are by and large the bad stuff. More and more supermarkets are likely to offer an organic option, or at least ones not administered hormones and antibiotics, and they might be willing to order more if enough customers ask for it. Try talking to your store's in-house butcher or manager if you want better meat and poultry options. You might be pleasantly surprised. If your store isn't willing to stock your needs, head elsewhere. Traditional stand-alone butcher shops and, you guessed it, farmers' markets are more likely to stock the better stuff, and often the great stuff.

THINGS TO DO AND QUESTIONS TO ASK WHEN BUYING MEAT

The following suggestions come from Jessica Applestone, co-owner with her husband, Joshua, the butcher, of Fleisher's Grass-fed and Organic Meats in Kingston, New York (Fleishers.com). She contends that if you ask enough questions, you can find someone raising animals well anywhere in the country.

1. **Decide what you're looking for.**
What are your limitations? Do you care more about how humanely the animals are raised or about what the animals eat? Are you

looking only for local? Only organic? Only (fully) pastured? Or 100 percent grass-fed?

2. Go to the farm.

Visit the place where your animals come from. Many people who sell at farmers' markets allow farm visits. A farmer with nothing to hide should welcome you, and should usually want to and be able to sell you meat directly. "When you're on the farm you want quiet. Noisy animals mean there are problems. You want something relatively clean, but it's not going to be Old MacDonald's," says Applestone. "It's still muddy, there are still flies and manure. But there shouldn't be an ammonia smell that knocks you out when you open the chicken coop. Animals do not look like they do at the county fair, but that doesn't mean it's inhumane."

3. To be sure that you're getting organic, make sure the sellers have a certificate.

If someone claiming to be certified organic doesn't have their certification on display at their market stall, don't buy from them. Ask them to bring the certificate the following week. If they give you a hassle, something's wrong. They've paid good money for the certification and should want to show it off. Remember there's no such thing as "natural" certification.

4. If you want 100 percent grass-fed, do two things.

First, pay attention to the season. Frozen grass-fed can be available year-round, but fresh grass-fed is a seasonal product. Second, look at the color of the fat. Entirely grass-fed animals have yellow fat. If the animal has eaten any grain at all, the fat will be white.

5. Make friends with your slaughterhouse.

This may not be possible for most consumers, but if it is, go for it. Or frequent a butcher shop that is friendly with its slaughterhouse.

THE LIST: WHERE TO SHOP FOR MEAT
A sliding scale of choices from best to worst

- Farmers' markets, CSA meat shares, and butcher shops specializing in well-sourced local grass-fed and organic meat. To find these, look them up online or ask trusted locavore friends or sustainably minded restaurateurs for advice on finding the purest market stalls and butchers. And always ask questions when shopping (see page 58).
- Health food stores, bigger natural-food-store chains like Whole Foods, websites, and butcher shops that carry some organic meat
- Supermarkets that carry some conscious options with managers who are willing to take your suggestions and answer your questions

AVOID: Supermarkets and big-box chain stores that don't carry any organic food, or that sell mainly frozen meat and boxed conventional beef patties

These are the people who know the secrets of what every animal eats—they open their guts. Applestone's guys have told her tales of finding plastic bags and candy wrappers (though not, thankfully, in her animals). Apparently it's not an uncommon thing for farmers to go to factories and load up on candy or packaged sliced bread and bulk the animals up on it, plastic and all. I wouldn't eat this stuff, and I certainly don't want my food eating it, either.

6. Expect a different product.
Grass-fed and organic meat doesn't have the taste and uniformity of flavor and texture that U.S. consumers have come to expect with feedlot animals. It varies according to the breed and pasture on which the animal was raised. The crucial thing when cooking

grass-fed meat is not to overcook it; it's a lean protein and can become tough more quickly than conventional meat. When properly cooked, it should not be chewy or overly gamey. If it is, find another farmer.

MARKET SCARES

Whenever consumers are opting to seek out (and sometimes pay more for) something they deem safer, there are always going to be detractors waiting in the wings to catch the purer producers doing something wrong. Blue Hill's Dan Barber refers to this as "doing gotcha" with the farmers. More than a few newspaper articles of late have taken to calling foul on organics and even on farmers' market vendors. One could argue that their energy would be a lot better spent reporting on, investigating, and outing the horrors of our industrial food supply, which are gargantuan compared to the occasional untrustworthy small farmer. I have mixed feelings when I read a gotcha article about a local meat guy who turns out to be subcontracting animals to his neighbors, when the rules of the market he sells at prohibit this practice. On the one hand, I'm glad for the information so I can vote with my dollars and buy elsewhere. Trust is absolutely crucial, especially in the

tip

Don't forget other meats. Look beyond your everyday offerings for eco-friendly options such as bison, deer, goat, rabbit, and more. Wild animals like deer are part of the natural carbon cycle. Bison (otherwise known as buffalo) have been eating across—and not overgrazing—prairie grasses for thousands of years. For the purest farmed bison, look for the USDA and National Bison Association's Certified American Buffalo seal, which indicates the animal wasn't given unneeded antibiotics or growth hormones or fed animal by-products. Small animals have less of a footprint than big ones. Rabbit in particular is a sustainable meat that can be raised on small farms with minimal environmental impact. They're said to produce more meat per equal amounts of water and feed than cattle. Check out EatWild.com and BisonCentral.com for where to buy the purest versions.

DON'T HAVE A FARMERS' MARKET?

Order meat online—many farms now send organic meat through the mail, or sell a whole animal (butchered or not) to friends wanting to share. Try to support farms closest to you. Some sources:

The American Pastured Poultry Producers Association: APPPA.org
EatWild.com
FoodRoutes.org
FarmToTable.org
AMS.USDA.gov/farmersmarkets
LocalHarvest.org

uncertified natural/local realm. If we can't believe the very sort of farmer who bases his entire reputation on being trustworthy, the whole system could fall apart very quickly. But, on the other hand, one rotten local egg is just that. I don't let it turn me off of what I know to be a better alternative to factory farming. Americans have more access to legitimately sustainable clean food right now than ever before. "The world is pretty transparent if you're going to the farmers' market," says Dan Barber. "It's not perfect, but they do a pretty good job with the regulation."

NAVIGATING THE SUPERMARKET

There will inevitably come a moment when you will find your-self in a supermarket—even if you have access to a meat CSA, a good butcher, or a farmers' markets—confused and trying to make sense of the numerous meat options. The best thing to do in these surroundings is get over the sticker shock and opt for USDA organic. If there's no organic, start reading labels. Many stores—even big-box chain stores like Wal-Mart—now carry nonorganic

THE LIST: MEAT

A sliding scale of choices from best to worst

- Local/organic and local/sustainable offerings from a small farmer or a butcher you trust
- Organic but not local, preferably pastured
- Certified Humane
- Meat carrying labels you now know to be somewhat meaningful, especially if you've contacted the farmer or producer to ask any questions you might have

AVOID: Conventional meat from factory farms (even if it's labeled "natural")

"natural" brands, some even from Certified Humane family (as opposed to factory) farms. It's easiest to just walk out with whatever the store might carry, but don't get lazy! Remember, you are what the animal you're eating ate.

When shopping in a supermarket, make sure you ask the butcher

RATIONALIZING THE COST

Yes, nonconventionally raised animals—organic or otherwise—are more expensive than regular old supermarket meat (though not actually more than fancy cuts at a high-end butcher). But now that you know what cheap meat really is, you won't want to spend any money on it at all. You know you're paying extra for so many benefits, not just a tasty steak (though that's certainly a big one). And you'll be in good conscious consumer company: According to the market research firm Mintel, sales of organic meat increased tenfold in a five-year period, from $33 million in 2002 to $364 million in 2007. You can offset the price difference by consuming less meat.

how the meat they're selling was "decontaminated" at the slaughter-house. Lovely thought, right? But absolutely worth knowing about, because apparently most conventional chickens—and even some "natural" conventional chickens—are dunked in a chlorine bath as part of their bulk slaughter. I won't use chlorine bleach to clean my home (see chapter ten), and certainly don't want to ingest its residue. I'm not alone. In 2007, when Britain was considering lifting a ban against importing U.S. chicken, their newspapers were calling for

EATING WHOLE HOG

Have you heard the phrase "Honor the protein?" It's a bit hokey, yes, but what it sums up is important. Now that you've done your meat homework and are spending more money and eating less, you'll want to get the most out of what you buy. Not just for economic reasons, but to honor the animal that gave its life for your dinner, to offset whatever strain it already put on the environment, and to reduce waste. Even though I'm not a vegetarian, I still think about the animal behind my pork chops. There's nothing more dishonorable than rendering a slaughtered-for-you animal inedible by cooking it poorly, or not using all of it. If you're a master butcher, this might mean buying the whole hog and eating it nose to tail. (For help on that, check out the British chef Fergus Henderson's books, *The Whole Beast: Nose to Tail Eating* and *Beyond Nose to Tail: More Omnivorous Recipes for the Adventurous Cook.* You can also look for the many, many blogs Henderson has inspired.) For those of us who don't wish to eat pig's tail, or consider offal—hearts, brains, stomachs, and other organs—awful, this could just mean making stock whenever you have leftover bones. Meat leftovers can easily be incorporated into sandwiches, curries, hashes, shepherd's pies, and soups. Every scrap can and should be used. This also means ordering meat wisely and buying sustainable cuts. Did you know there is only one hangar steak per steer? That's why you'll rarely find them at a small butcher shop. A good butcher should be able to tell you how to cook any cut with tasty results, even ones you're not familiar with.

labels to be stuck on our poultry that would read "Treated with Anti-microbial Substances" or "Decontaminated by Chemicals." Obviously no one wants their birds or steaks to come with salmonella, *E. coli*, campylobacter, and listeria, but chlorine baths are banned for meat in the European Union. In the United States, these baths are permitted for poultry as well as for conventionally grown salad mixes, meat, and more, but the practice is banned for all certified organic food. There are also a few nonorganic U.S. companies employing the chlorine-free processing techniques used in Europe. Alternative disinfectants include ozone (this is also used in European swimming pools) and electrolyzed "eco water" (Murray's Chicken, a Certified Humane, family farmed, and widely available brand around New York, uses this). Air-chilled birds, which are what is mainly sold at Whole Foods, are hung separately, out of water, so they don't cross-contaminate. This eliminates the need for a disinfectant.

Spend a few minutes *now* to figure out what the best poultry and meat options are in your local stores. Call up the managers and ask them what they sell and do some quick Internet research on the brands. Knowledge means never having to stand dazed in front of the shrink-wrapped bloody parts again, feeling like you're playing Russian roulette.

EATING OUT

When rethinking meat, don't forget about what you find in restaurants. Do. Not. Eat. Fast. Food. There is no fast food joint that serves truly 100 percent sustainable meat, though you may run across some "naturally raised" meat. When out, you might want to avoid ordering meat, or frequent spots that you know source their meat well. This involves asking even more questions, and it's no

GOOD RESTAURANTS

To find restaurants serving well-sourced meat, ask your locavore friends, trusted butcher, or farmers' market vendor. And check out these sites:

DineGreen.com

LocalHarvest.org/restaurants

OrganicHighways.com

OrganicKitchen.com/rest/rest.html

OrganicFoodDatabase.net

time to be shy. Jessica Applestone of Fleisher's has eaten in restaurants that claimed on their menus to serve her own meat, when she knew that they were no longer ordering from her—and even more suspect was that their former orders were minimal. Maybe only the pork used to be from Fleisher's, but their name on the menu implies that all of the meat served comes from them. This highlights an unfortunate truth about eating out: Just because a restaurant uses organic eggs on their brunch menu doesn't mean the eggs used in everything else from baked goods to hollandaise sauce are also organic.

I have locavore friends who have decided that all bets are off when at restaurants—they just order and eat whatever they want. My personal rule is that I must know the producer of the meat or really trust the butcher or the chef who is selling or serving me the meat; otherwise I don't eat it, even when "eating out" at a friend's home. By and large I'm a vegetarian when out and about.

CHAPTER FOUR

dairy and eggs

Once you've gotten a line on where to get clean meat, finding similar versions of other animal products—eggs, cheese, yogurt, milk, and all of the tasty things you can make from them—will be pretty easy to do. While the good stuff is more widely available in regular supermarkets and local shops than good meat is, the even better stuff tends to be available at farmers' markets, farms, and via CSAs.

EGGS

Which came first? The free-range chicken or the free-range egg? For once there is an answer: The chicken—as discussed in chapter three, only chickens can be called "free range" under USDA regulations. The best eggs come from the best chickens, and you already know how to find those. As with poultry, your best options are, in order beginning with the best: local, pastured, and organic; local, pastured, and sustainable; and organic. Avoid conventional.

Many egg cartons are covered with labels indicating what the chickens ate, if they were able to roam, and if antibiotics were administered. These claims have varying degrees of truth

MORE ON EGGS

- To find the freshest supermarket eggs, look for the "pack date" number on the carton—a three-digit code representing the day of the year (365, for example, would be December 31) when the eggs went into the carton. This date is generally a few days after the egg was laid, and the "sell by" date must be less than 45 days from the "pack date." At a farmers' market, just ask when they were laid.

- If your eggs don't have a sell-by date—these are state mandated, and not all states require them—there are other ways of sussing out age. Older eggs contain more air than fresh ones: Put them in water and they'll float, or shake them (gently) and you'll hear a noise. Or crack them open: A cloudy white is very fresh; a clear one is aging. You want to use your eggs within three to five weeks after purchase. If they have gone bad, you'll smell it.

- Manufacturers pay to have their eggs voluntarily USDA-graded (AA and so on). Government regulations require that these be "carefully washed and sanitized using special detergent." Most detergents aren't something you want near your food, let alone your counters (see chapter ten). For conventional eggs, this likely means chlorine, an ammonium compound, or iodine, among other things. For organic eggs, it could mean chlorine at an extremely low level, or other disinfectants like hydrogen peroxide or even vinegar. Some small producers may "dry clean" eggs, using a brush or sandpaper. To avoid harsh detergents, opt for organic and/or farmers' market eggs.

- Pastured chickens eating a natural diet of worms and grubs make eggs with intensely yellow—almost orange—yolks. If your farmers' market pastured eggs have pale yolks, question your farmer. To find pastured eggs near you, check out EatWild.com.

- Choose paperboard egg cartons over plastic or Styrofoam, and don't toss them when you've gone through the dozen. Farmers at markets will reuse them. Tuck empties into your market bags so you won't forget them when you go.

to them, but actually can point you in the direction of the purest eggs. If you're shopping at a supermarket, you should be able to find organic eggs, and some big chains even have in-house organic brands. Farmers' market eggs from pastured hens will likely come in all sorts of beautiful shapes, colors (shell color is based on hen breed), and sizes—much less uniform looking than their industrial counterparts.

If you have any questions regarding how the chickens that laid your eggs were raised or what they were fed (see page 57 for what they should and shouldn't be eating), ask the farmer or supermarket manager directly, or call the company listed on the carton. Then poach, boil, and bake with abandon. Bonus: Eggs are a lower-impact way of eating animal protein.

MILK

When my daughter began drinking cow in addition to breast milk, I decided to revisit the odd world of milk. We had already been drinking organic moo juice (mainly in coffee) to avoid rBGH (recombinant bovine growth hormone, also known as rBST—recombinant bovine somatotropin) and antibiotics. Apparently I hadn't been considering all there was to consider. While I don't drink conventional milk (and suggest you don't either), there are many options available in the eco-realm other than just organic. And not all organic milks are the same. These choices boil down to a not-so-simple list: organic milk from factory farms (see page 25); organic milk from farm collectives; organic milk from grass-fed cows (local and not); nonorganic milk that is hormone free from grass-fed cows that receive antibiotics only if they're sick (local and not); the former two options but from grain-fed and possibly some grass-fed cows; farmers' market procurable milk; raw milk

OTHER ANIMAL MILKS?

Yes, I'm cow-centric, but I know other people are into goat and sheep's milk for different reasons. I don't happen to be. You can absolutely find great versions of these milks by following the same rules and using the exact same websites and resources I lay out for finding good cow's milk. To begin, query the market people and butchers you'd turn to for information on cattle. And go from there.

(unpasteurized and usually bought underground in buyers' clubs, as it's illegal in most states—see page 74); and so on.

On top of these basics (ha!), milk buyers can also consider ultrapasteurized versus lightly pasteurized, homogenized versus nonhomogenized, and packaging (glass bottles versus cartons versus plastic).

PASTEURIZATION

This is the process of heating milk to various high temperatures for varying lengths of time to kill off potentially harmful bacteria and to extend shelf life. During this process some flavor and nutrients are also destroyed. Raw milk, which is not pasteurized, contains the highest levels of nutrients, but might also harbor bacteria and must be sourced meticulously. Pasteurization times and temperatures are regulated by the government and are based on the purity, fat content, and concentration of the milk, among other things.

ULTRAPASTEURIZED

Ultrapasteurized milk (UHT) has been heated to a very high temperature—a minimum of 280°F—for at least two seconds. This makes for a long shelf life, but ultrapasteurized milk has

THE LIST: MILK
A sliding scale of choices from best to worst

- Lightly pasteurized, grass-fed local, certified organic; and/or lightly pasteurized, grass-fed local, sustainable (not administered hormones or antibiotics). Glass bottles are preferable to cardboard cartons, which are preferable to plastic.
- Same as above, but from cows fed a mix of grass and grain
- Certified organic, lightly pasteurized (if not available, then ultra-pasteurized), grass-fed (if not available, grass- and grain-fed), from small family dairies that aren't local
- Certified organic, lightly pasteurized (if not available, then ultra-pasteurized) from bigger producers

AVOID: Conventional milk. If it's your only choice, call the producer and ask questions. You should disagree with how they raise their animals and what they feed them, but there are some producers in this realm who at least don't administer hormones to their animals.

diminished nutrients and not much flavor. If you see a sell-by date a month or more from the day you're shopping, you'll know that milk was ultrapasteurized.

LIGHTLY OR LOW PASTEURIZED
This seems like a good compromise between raw and UHT. "Lightly" or "low" is used to distinguish pasteurized milk from the increasingly ubiquitous ultrapasteurized product. It's heated using a method called "high temperature short time" (HTST), which tends to be done at 161°F for about 15 seconds but varies by producer. At the time of my research, Natural by Nature (see page 71), an organic grass-fed milk sold in and around Pennsylvania,

did their low pasteurization at 165°F, while Straus Creamery (StrausFamilyCreamery.com) in Northern California did theirs at 170°F for 19 seconds, and Hudson Valley Fresh (see page 73) did theirs at 164°F for 20 seconds. All of these temperatures adhere to government-set standards, and kill what needs to be killed while retaining flavor and some, but not all, nutrients.

tip

The organic watchdog group the Cornucopia Institute ranks organic dairy farms all over the country on their web-site. It's a must-consult list when searching for conscious milk—goat, cow, or sheep: Cornucopia.org/dairysurvey/index.html. Also Eat Wild's all grass-fed list is helpful: EatWild.com/products/allgrassdairies.html.

HOMOGENIZATION

The process of breaking up fat molecules in cream to such a small size that they remain suspended evenly in milk rather than separating out is called homogenization. It's why most milk doesn't have separate cream on top. Purists don't like homogenized milk; it's too processed. I might agree with them, except I have yet to find a nonhomogenized milk that foams well using my espresso machine. Ultrapasteurized milk also falls flat. Priorities!

Local Milk

It may sound like sourcing a local and certified organic milk, or a local and sustainable, grass-fed, lightly pasteurized milk, sold in glass bottles, is a needle-in-a-haystack process. It's not, especially with a little compromise on feed (sometimes the cows eat a little grain), organic status (some good local dairies are sustainable and don't administer hormones, but do administer antibiotics if they absolutely have to, and therefore aren't certified organic), and packaging (one milk I love flavor-wise comes in plastic). My current four favorite local milks all involve some level of compromise (see opposite), but none of them is ultrapasteurized. These

SOME OF MY CURRENT FAVORITE MILK PRODUCERS

Milk Thistle: mainly grass-fed, certified organic, lightly pasteurized, some homogenized (reduced fat), some not (whole), local milk sold in glass bottles at farmers' markets and at least one Whole Foods near me. MilkThistleFarm.com.

Ronnybrook: mainly grass-fed, sustainable, and no administered hormones, but not certified organic, pasteurized (but not ultra) local milk sold in glass bottles at farmers' markets and other shops around the region, and at their Manhattan retail store. Ronnybrook.com.

Hudson Valley Fresh: mainly grass-fed, sustainable, and no administered hormones, but not certified organic, lightly pasteurized milk from a local nonprofit dairy cooperative, bottled in the town where my parents have a house. Unfortunately it comes in plastic bottles. Available at various stores in the region and at several cafés near me. I'm addicted to milky cappuccinos and this froths and foams like no other milk I've ever tried. HudsonValleyFresh.com.

Natural by Nature: I tend to shop for milk at farmers' markets and specialty stores. This is my go-to milk-in-a-carton when I'm shopping at the health food store. It's low pasteurized, certified organic, from grass-fed cows on family farms in southeastern Pennsylvania. Their website details precisely how not all USDA certified organic milk is the same, and how they go beyond organic standards. It's sweet, clean, and rich tasting. Natural-by-Nature.com.

brands are available only in my region; there's no such thing as a good local milk distributed all over the country. But similar milks can absolutely be found near you. Poke around where you live—ask for it at farmers' markets, at butcher and cheese shops that carry local products, and read labels at health food stores and supermarkets. Where there's grass-fed beef, there's likely grass-fed milk. "Local" takes on new meaning when it comes to the freshest milk—my milk comes from the cow to me in about thirty-six hours versus a week plus for supermarket milk. Live near a farm? Maybe you can snag it day of. You'll never go back to your old ways.

Raw Milk

I've read many compelling cases for drinking raw milk, most notably by Nina Planck. If raw milk interests you, pick up a copy of her book, *Real Food*, as well as *The Untold Story of Milk: Green Pastures, Contented Cows, and Raw Dairy Foods* by Ron Schmid. The crux of the argument is that unpasteurized milk contains very valuable and unique nutrients, and that good raw milk from well-maintained cows isn't any more likely to be contaminated by dangerous bacteria like salmonella, *E. coli*, and listeria than pasteurized milk from conventional factory-farm cows. If I lived in a

HOW TO FIND RAW MILK AND OTHER DAIRY

If raw milk isn't legal where you live, you can drive to where it is legal, or even have it flown in from California, but these options aren't environmentally friendly. Instead, ask around, check out RealMilk.com, and/or contact your local Weston A. Price Foundation chapter at WestonAPrice.org/localchapters. The foundation is dedicated to restoring nutrient-dense foods to the human diet through education, research, and activism. If you locate a buyers' club you want to join, Nina Planck has an excellent list of safety-related questions to ask any raw milk farmer on her website, NinaPlanck.com.

If you're thinking of feeding raw milk to a young child because of its unique nutrients, *you* should be the guinea pig. Small and developing systems are more susceptible to the potential dangers of unpasteurized milk. Drink some first and wait twenty-four hours before filling kids' sippy cups. Keep in mind that this is not a foolproof test; raw milk that doesn't bother your system may affect a child differently.

state where raw milk was legal to buy in stores, had my own cow, or lived closer to a farm that sold raw, I'd likely drink raw. But currently I don't. While raw milk is legal in some states, in others, including New York state, it's permitted to be sold only on site at a few farms. Other states ban it entirely. Regulations change not infrequently. To check the legal status of raw milk where you live, go to RealMilk.com/happening.html.

The previous paragraph isn't one I'd even be writing if I lived in, say, France. If you've visited France, you've surely had raw milk, especially in the form of a delicious, stinky cheese. For now, my compromise is lightly pasteurized. There are aged raw milk cheeses that are permitted across the board in the United States and I choose those whenever I find them.

tip

If you have a child who—ahem—covets her friends' blue Popsicles, pour plain organic yogurt (we love Hawthorne Valley—HawthorneValleyFarm.org) into Popsicle molds; "color" with frozen blueberries or mashed raspberries; maybe add a little organic molasses; freeze; and voilà: Popsicles whenever she wants them. Offer them at particularly exciting and odd times of day when dessert would never be permitted, like breakfast. Why not? They're good for you.

YOGURT

The issues with yogurt are the same as with milk. And there are almost as many interesting small yogurt producers around as there are milk producers. Generally speaking, it can be hard to find good plain yogurt. It's worth seeking out, as most yogurts available are loaded with unbelievable amounts of sugar—much more than you'd ever suspect. And the myriad yogurt things marketed to kids! I hope everyone out there knows full well that a cartoon-character-bedecked plastic tube of unnaturally blue yogurt that goes into the freezer cannot possibly be healthful, even if it's certified organic! As Marion Nestle writes in *What to Eat*: "Some fruit-flavored yogurts actually have fruit in them, but caveat emptor: Most have more sugar than fruit, and many have no real fruit at all—just fruit concentrates, added colors to make them look fruitier, and thickeners (flour, corn starch, pectin, and carrageenan) to hold them together." I'm also not thrilled with the

DIY YOGURT

Yogurt is easy to make—neither a yogurt-maker nor a special culture is necessary. The final product may be thinner in consistency than commercial yogurt. This recipe is from Sally Fallon's cookbook *Nourishing Traditions*. Fallon is also the president of the Weston A. Price Foundation.

Makes 1 quart

1/2 cup good-quality commercial plain yogurt, or 1/2 cup yogurt from previous batch

1 quart pasteurized whole milk, nonhomogenized

a candy thermometer

Gently heat the milk to 180°F and allow to cool to about 110°F. Stir in the yogurt, and pour the mixture into a shallow glass, enamel, or stainless-steel container. Cover the container and place in a warm oven (about 150°F, or a gas oven with a pilot light) overnight. In the morning, transfer to the refrigerator. Throughout the day, use a clean kitchen towel to mop up any whey that exudes from the yogurt. Keeps for a couple of weeks.

plastic packaging certain brands of yogurt come in (for more on plastics, see chapter eight).

In general, look for yogurt from a local organic dairy you trust. The yogurt should have a minuscule ingredient list—all that should be listed is milk and some bacteria strains. Buying a big tub of it, instead of little individual servings, is a more economical and environmentally friendly choice, especially if your town recycles the kind of plastic the container is made of. Then, if you want to add fruit or sweetener, you're in control of how much and what gets used.

BUTTER, ICE CREAM, BUTTERMILK, CREAM, ETC.

It goes without saying that all of the extra goodies made from cows and other milk-producing animals should be as pure as the milk and yogurt described here. Any store or market that stocks your favorite milk and yogurt is likely to have a good selection of butters. For all of your baking needs, look for sticks from the organic/local/grass-fed producers you buy your milk from. For daily spreading, taste through offerings from local farms and the beautiful hormone- and antibiotic-free butters at your favorite cheese shop. The freezer section at these very stores is where you want to be looking for your ice cream. There are plenty of organic versions—and even some local cold creamy goodness—available. Some are better than others, and some are purer than others. Read ingredient lists to find the best versions with no (or the fewest) additives; you should be able to recognize all of the ingredients, and the list should be very short. Even organic ice cream can have some unpronounceable emulsifiers you might choose to avoid.

Still, organic is your best option to avoid hormones, anything genetically modified, and more. Within the conventional arena, there exists a line of ice creams with a mercifully short ingredient list: Häagen-Dazs five. It's named after the number of ingredients in the ice cream and based on one of the author Michael Pollan's seven rules for eating: "Don't eat anything with more than five ingredients, or ingredients you can't pronounce." Milk, cream, sugar, eggs, and one flavor are all pronounceable and understandable. But they're also all preferable in organic and/or sustainable versions.

CHEESE

Perhaps the most important animal product on earth, to my mind, is cheese. Talk about food pleasure! Happily, most farmers' markets and cheese stores, or even some grocery store cheese counters these days, have handmade specimens that are not only fabulous

---

GOING EUROPEAN

Some people buy only foreign cheese because they believe standards enforced by European governments, like the French AOC (*appellation d'origine contrôlée*) and the Italian DOC (*denominazione di origine controllata*), guarantee a product that has had minimal exposure to pesticides and antibiotics. This is a misunderstanding. While it's true that the growth hormone rBGH is banned in Italy and France, not all European cheeses are made with regionally sourced milk. AOC and DOC only ensure the cheese is made in a way that preserves and protects its traditional character and specific recipe. If the standards of one cheese require that it be made only with grass-fed milk from a specific region, you might be in the clear. But that's pretty rare. One exception: real Parmesan. The beneficial bacteria needed to create traditional DOC Parmigiano-Reggiano are thrown off by antibiotics, so if it is allowed to be called Parmigiano-Reggiano, it's antibiotic free. But unless you live in Italy, it still has to travel quite a journey to your table.

---

but pure. I may not like to drink goat and sheep's milk, but I sure do love them in cheese form. People who work at cheese counters generally like to talk cheese. Ask questions to find the local ones and to make sure what you're getting is the quality you want (no hormones or antibiotics, grass-fed or from animals that were fed some organic feed). Take recommendations and taste copiously.

If your only concern here is avoiding pesticides, hormones, and antibiotics, your local supermarket should carry some sort of fine-for-melting USDA certified organic cheese that comes enshrouded in plastic. If they don't yet, ask for it. If you're lucky, it won't taste like wax or come preshredded from a factory-farm dairy operation. This isn't meant to sound elitist, but there's a difference between mass-produced supermarket cheese and stinky, runny, nutty, chalky, fabulous handcrafted cheeses. One quite tasty supermarket-available variety (depending on where you live) is Organic Valley. Their Muenster and cheddar ooze temptingly between pieces of grilled bread.

tip

Buy hunks of real Parmigiano-Reggiano, not the pre-grated stuff. When you've shaved your way to the end, save the rind to use as a Parmesan bouillon of sorts to flavor soups. It's a great way to get extra use and delicious flavor out of something that would otherwise be tossed in the trash.

seafood

IN A CONSCIOUS KITCHEN, NOTHING IS MORE CHALLENGING and confusing than seafood. Despite the fact that fish is highly touted as a lean protein and a great source of heart-healthy omega-3 fatty acids, it's arguably more toxic than anything else we eat because of what we've done to our waterways. Think about it in the most basic, unscientific, commonsense terms: Our oceans, rivers, lakes, and ponds are like a sewer system of all of the environmentally destructive things on the planet. Chemicals sprayed on land make their way into water as runoff, or by seeping down into the groundwater. Factories illegally dump their waste into water. Air particle pollution settles in water and stays there for a very long time. And everything we pour down drains—from pharmaceuticals to cleaning products to hormone-disrupting cosmetic residues—gets into our water supply. Some of these toxins have managed to "feminize" wild male fish: They develop female sex characteristics and are even able to grow eggs. And they're dining on broken-down pieces of plastic garbage that has made its way into the water.

Ingesting seafood from these waters is a health hazard. So much so that there are government seafood advisories that detail which fish and shellfish are safe to eat, in what quantities, and at what phases of our lives (the pregnant and the young are particularly vulnerable).

Our government does not issue similar warnings about poultry or livestock, even conventionally raised animals fed the worst possible feed. I'm sure the meat we eat—organic or otherwise—also contains toxins, especially if the animal it came from grazed near a smog-spewing coal plant. But that these advisories are seafood- and waterway-specific puts everything in a different light.

Beyond health hazards, there are a couple of other crucial things to consider regarding fish and shellfish. First is sustainability: We have overfished our waterways in an environmentally destructive fashion. Consumers need to be educated to find sustainable wild seafood caught in less environmentally destructive ways. Second are the hazards of aquaculture (the seafood equivalent of agriculture, aka farmed seafood). Farming should be the cure for overfished waterways, but it isn't. A few farmed options are eco-okay (mollusks, for example; see the Environmental Defense Fund's suggestions on page 90 for more), but most farmed seafood is the equivalent of conventional factory-farmed animals in terms of what it's fed, how it's kept, and the environmental burden it creates.

A note of encouragement: "There is plenty of good fish to eat that you can feel good about from a health and sustainability perspective. It does take some education," says Laura Pagano, a staff attorney for the Natural Resources Defense Council's oceans program (NRDC. org/oceans). So here's an education, starting with the toxins, moving on to the sustainability issues, and ending with shopping advice.

THE BIGGEST TOXIN ISSUES

Both the regulation of toxins and the actual toxin levels in our waterways change at such a dizzying rate that seafood information gets outdated very quickly, so it's imperative to stay abreast of it online.

Pollutants—and affected species—vary region by region, river by lake by pond by ocean. If you're buying local seafood, it's crucial to familiarize yourself with what the issues are near you (EPA.gov/waterscience/fish/states.htm), or—if you're not buying local—what the issues are with regard to the fish you like to eat the most and the places they come from. Mercury and polychlorinated biphenyls (PCBs) are two of the most significant and far-reaching contaminant issues:

tip

Don't toss your bulbs!
The amount of mercury in a compact fluorescent lightbulb—or a thermometer—is arguably pretty small, but you still shouldn't toss them in the garbage. The mercury sent to landfills will eventually work its way into the waterways. To dispose of these items properly, follow the EPA guidelines for hazardous waste: EPA.gov/ epawaste/hazard/ wastetypes/universal/ lamps. Some big-box stores like IKEA and Home Depot collect them for recycling. Check with stores near you.

MERCURY

This naturally occurring element is a neurotoxin, meaning it can damage the brain and nervous system. Beyond natural sources, it's in our fish, thanks to emissions from coal-fired power plants that make their way into our waterways and accumulate in fish flesh. Some industries also dump waste containing mercury into our water. All seafood likely contains some mercury, but the seafood highest on the food chain—big predator fish like shark, swordfish, king mackerel, tilefish, and tuna that eat smaller fish—contain the highest levels. I avoid these completely even though advisories say seafood with mercury can be eaten in moderation. How much is said to be safe to eat depends on your age and sex: Older kids can ostensibly eat more than younger kids, and women of reproductive age and especially pregnant women have to be extremely careful eating fish containing mercury, as it crosses the placenta and can harm a developing brain. Government

CANNED TUNA

The tuna in cans is preferable to fresh tuna because it tends to come from smaller tuna species, which contain lower levels of mercury. This is especially true of canned light tuna, which is primarily from smallish skipjack tunas. Unfortunately, it's rare that a can will identify the exact fish it contains, and skipjack isn't primarily fished with environmentally friendly gear. Still, it—and canned wild Alaskan salmon—are touted as great inexpensive safer fish options, especially for people who live far from water. To locate the best canned tuna, do the research before hitting the store and eat in moderation, since many cans are lined with harmful chemicals like bisphenol-A (BPA; see page 155). Vital Choice (VitalChoice.com) says there is no BPA in their tuna, mackerel, sardine, or salmon cans. I've also seen tuna in glass jars, which are safer than cans. If you're trying to be a locavore, canned tuna, like fresh tuna, may present a food miles issue.

advisories on frequency and amounts deemed allowable and at what phase of life keep changing (and often are politically motivated). The short answer is that no amount of mercury is desirable. There are (for now) other fish in the sea, so choose something else. Recent media tales of sushi-addicted celebrities with mercury poisoning drive this commonsense approach home.

POLYCHLORINATED BIPHENYLS (PCBS)
Unlike mercury, there are no natural sources of PCBs, a family of chemicals deemed "probably carcinogenic" by the EPA and the International Agency for Research on Cancer (IARC). According to the Department of Health and Human Services Agency for Toxic Substances and Disease Registry, PCBs are "Mixtures of up to 209 individual chlorinated compounds [that] . . . have been used as coolants and lubricants in transformers, capacitors, and other electrical equipment because they don't burn easily and are good

tip

Some good ways to avoid toxins: Don't eat seafood daily, and don't eat too much of any one species. To avoid mercury, eat smaller fish. To avoid PCBs, eat less fatty fish (unfortunately, fish containing the highest levels of omega-3s are also likely to have elevated PCB levels), and avoid seafood from areas—here and abroad—known to be polluted.

insulators. The manufacture of PCBs was stopped in the U.S. in 1977 because of evidence that they build up in the environment and can cause harmful health effects." They entered the air, water, and soil during their manufacture, use, and disposal, and remain there today, as well as in pre-1977 items like old fluorescent lighting fixtures. They're also still being released into the environment from hazardous-waste sites, especially from improper waste handling (disposal, leaks, incineration). PCBs accumulate in fish and marine mammals in levels reaching "many thousands of times higher than in water." In short, not something you want to be feeding you and yours for dinner. Farmed seafood also contains PCBs, at even higher concentrations than their wild counterparts; its feed usually includes ground-up wild fish, which contain, you guessed it, PCBs.

THE BIGGEST ENVIRONMENTAL CONCERNS

Wild and farmed seafood are two different creatures, so their environmental burdens beyond toxins are distinct, too.

Wild

The main environmental issues for wild seafood, ocean or freshwater, are sustainability and harvesting methods (how the fish was caught). A number of species are currently drastically overfished—cod has long been the poster child of a depleted fish, so much so

THE LIST: BEST FISHING METHODS
A sliding scale of options from best to worst
(Unfortunately, not many seafood options are labeled with how they were caught.)

- Hook and line, harpoon, scuba, and trolls
- More destructive methods include long lines, drift nets, ocean floor–disturbing bottom trawls (trawls are very different from trolls), and other nets that catch many unintended species, which then get thrown away

AVOID: Fish caught by the use of dynamite (fish are blasted out of coral reefs, destroying them) and cyanide (fish are stunned out of reefs). These are destructive and short-sighted ways of getting seafood.

that there have been cod fishing bans from the Northwest Atlantic to the Baltic Sea. Sharks, bluefin tuna, and many kinds of West Coast rockfish also are overfished, according to the Monterey Bay Aquarium Seafood Watch. What's been depleted can sometimes be renewed, so check online for the latest information. With regard to how fish are being caught, some methods are environmentally friendlier than others. To learn more about these, go to FishOnline .org/information/methods.

tip

Sportfishers beware! It feels conscious to catch and cook your own food. But sportsfish like northern pike, large-mouth bass, and yellow perch tend to be very contaminated. Always check EPA and local advisories prior to planning fishing trips.

Farmed

The main environmental issues for farmed fish and seafood—pollution and sustainability—are tightly linked to personal health concerns. Many fish farms, domestic and abroad, use feed that's similar to the gunk that factory-farmed animals are fed, including antibiotics and hormones, plus dyes (this is what makes farmed salmon as pink as its wild counterpart), and other undesirable additives. In 2009, a neurologist from the University of Louisville issued a warning in a paper published in the *Journal of Alzheimer's Disease* saying that farmed fish that were fed cow by-products could even be at risk for mad cow disease. Some fish, like tilapia, tend to be raised on vegetarian feed, so this wouldn't be an issue with them.

Farmed imports are particularly suspect, and 80 percent of our seafood is imported, mainly from Asia, with some coming from Central America. China is the world's largest exporter of farmed seafood. "The concern with the farmed imported seafood is chemicals and the fact that they are raised in sewage pits," says the NRDC's Laura Pagano.

Some farmed seafood is actually fed wild, sometimes overfished fish. Ironic. This further depletes the waterways and makes the finished product high in environmental toxins like PCBs. There are even well-meaning farmers attempting to raise so called "organic" shrimp who also raise purer farmed fish to feed their purer farmed shrimp. That sounds like an unanswerable riddle for the carbon footprint crunchers! Farmed fish raised in open-ocean net pens pollute the water with waste. Some, like salmon, have been known to escape their pens and harm their wild counterparts by eating their food and spreading disease, not to mention genetically altering the species by breeding with them. Farmed and wild salmon may seem like the same fish, but they are actually different.

tip

When you're in front of a fish counter or looking at a restaurant menu, if you don't have a safe seafood card in your wallet, whip out your phone! Text the Blue Ocean Institute's handy FishPhone—30644—with the word "fish" and the species you're looking to get information on, and they text you right back with environmental and health information, giving your choice a Red, Yellow, or Green light.

THE LIST: SEAFOOD
A sliding scale of choices from best to worst

Wild

• Sustainably caught from a boat or fishmonger you trust and/or from a Marine Stewardship Council Certified fishery (MSC.org), a fairly trustworthy certification program for sustainable seafood. Choose local only if your local waterways aren't too polluted; check EPA advisories at EPA.gov/waterscience/fish/states.htm. Look up all species in a safe seafood guide (see page 89).

AVOID: Anything lacking a COOL label; imported fish from China and other countries known to have contaminated waters or to harvest in an unsustainable fashion.

Farmed

• Seafood from farmers trying to raise in an "organic" or ecologically sound manner, who aren't administering hormones and antibiotics, and who are possibly even using vegetarian feed. MSC certification is also available for aquaculture farms. Look for it. Look up all species in a safe seafood guide (see page 89).

AVOID: Anything fed hormones, antibiotics, dyes, and feed containing animal by-products; anything lacking a COOL label or that is imported from countries known to have the most polluted farms.

HOW TO FIND GOOD SEAFOOD

Finding safe seafood is almost as tricky as navigating the environmental issues. Usually, when in doubt, consumers can choose certified organic products to know they're getting purer, more regulated food. But as of press time there were no USDA organic standards for fish and shellfish. These have long been in the works, with rumors of much infighting. When they eventually happen, they will be only for farmed seafood, as there is no way to standardize wild-caught seafood. Fish farms do need to clean up their act, but Consumers Union (the nonprofit publisher of *Consumer Reports*—ConsumersUnion.org) claims the current work-in-progress seafood recommendations fail to meet fundamental USDA organic principles for feed as well as environmental protection. One of the stickier issues is whether "organic" farmed seafood can eat wild feed, since wild fish cannot be certified organic. Other causes of the holdup in passing certified organic seafood standards have been that the industry finds them impossibly tough, and some environmentalists don't like the idea of fish farming at all. But it's pretty clear that wild-caught fish alone cannot satisfy consumer seafood demand. In the interim, the eco-pescavores' seafood of choice is sustainable wild, well caught, eaten in moderation.

tip

Sometimes working with local seafood means using more flavor or technique. "Our local halibut isn't as good as the Alaskan, but it's something we should be working with, so we do," says Ben Ford of Ford's Filling Station in Culver City, California. Pacific halibut is certified as a best environmental choice by the Marine Stewardship Council. Ford pairs seared filets with marinated baby leeks, sweet pea coulis, roasted garlic butter, and ham hock gelée.

SAFE SEAFOOD GUIDES

Consumers need all the help we can get at the fish counter. Did you know that "rockfish" can mean more than sixty different kinds of fish? That on the Pacific West Coast there are eighty-two different species of groundfish? More than forty different species can be called snapper—some are overfished, while others are hook-and-line caught and acceptable. At the time I was researching this book, American farmed tilapia was fine to eat,

ONLINE GUIDES

Check out these sites for fish substitution suggestions, safe sushi guides, quick-read best and worst choices lists, and information on the most widely available seafood choices. Remember to check back with your preferred guide from time to time, as regulations and water pollution concerns change not infrequently.

- Blue Ocean Institute's Seafood Guide: BlueOcean.org
- Consumers Union: Greener Choices.org
- Environmental Defense Fund's Seafood Selector: OceansAlive.org
- Food & Water Watch: Foodand WaterWatch.org
- Global Aquaculture Alliance: GAAlliance.org
- Monterey Bay Aquarium's Seafood Watch Program: MBAYAQ .org/seafoodwatch
- National Oceanic and Atmospheric Administration National Marine Fisheries Service: www .NMFS.NOAA.gov/fishwatch
- Seafood Choices Alliance: SeafoodChoices.org
- The Ocean Conservancy: Ocean Conservancy.org

but Asian tilapia was not. Longline and hook-and-line haddock were good, but trawled haddock was a no-no. Thankfully you don't need to have an encyclopedic mind to buy seafood, just a wallet card printed from an encyclopedic database. Many of the environmental groups that are pushing for safer waterways, eco-friendlier wild fishing, and better aquaculture standards maintain such user-friendly databases (see above).

WHERE TO SHOP

Armed with the above guides, or a cell phone ready to text Fish-Phone, a consumer is ready to face any seafood counter. To further your chances of finding good fish, choose that counter wisely. This will depend heavily on where in the country you live. Knowledge-able scientists and chefs say to buy only from small, well-managed fisheries. Keep in mind that the pure stuff isn't cheap. As with meat, eating less fish, and less often, is more.

If you live near a Whole Foods, shop there. Their seafood is third-party certified and sustainable, and they work with the Marine Stewardship Council—look for the label to be sure you're

---

ENVIRONMENTAL DEFENSE FUND'S SEAFOOD SELECTOR

EDF maintains an extensive ecologically oriented database of safe seafood choices, and below are some of their best and worst choices. Check online for more, and for changes and updates at OceansAlive.org. If you're of reproductive age or are feeding children, look through the guides listed on page 89 to find the most up-to-date health-oriented information.

"ECO-BEST"

Fish

Char, Arctic (farmed)
Sablefish (Alaska, Canada)
Salmon, wild (Alaska)
Sardines, Pacific (U.S.)
Trout, rainbow (farmed)
Tuna, albacore (U.S., Canada)

Shellfish

Crab, Dungeness
Mussels
Oysters (farmed)
Shrimp, pink (Oregon)

"ECO-OK"

Fish

Cod, Pacific (trawl)
Flounder/sole (Pacific)
Squid; tilapia (Latin America)
Tuna, canned light

Shellfish

Clams (wild)
Crab, snow/tanner
Lobster, American/Maine
Scallops, sea (U.S., Canada)
Shrimp (U.S. wild)

"ECO-WORST"

Fish

Chilean sea bass
Grouper
Orange roughy
Rockfish (trawl)
Salmon, farmed/Atlantic
Shark
Swordfish (imported)
Tilefish (Gulf of Mexico/South Atlantic)
Tuna, bigeye/yellowfin (imported longline)
Tuna, bluefin

GREENPEACE'S SUPERMARKET SCORECARD

In the 2009 edition of this consumer-friendly scorecard, based on what seafood supermarkets stock and who they buy from, some big chains were singled out for doing well. These included Wegmans, Ahold (Stop & Shop, Giant), Whole Foods, Target, Safeway, Harris Teeter, and even Wal-Mart. Not so good? Winn-Dixie, Price Chopper, and Trader Joe's. See the full, most up-to-date list at Greenpeace.org.

getting what you want. They say their farmed options are free of artificial growth hormones, antibiotics, and preservatives, and are given feed free of poultry and mammalian by-products and genetically modified or cloned seafood. Don't shop blindly; ask questions, even in "good" stores. Don't live near a Whole Foods or one of the Greenpeace-approved markets (see sidebar, above)? Use the "Online Guides" listed on page 89 to get to know a few species you like and you know are safe, and shop exclusively for those no matter where you are. Like scallops? Memorize that scallops farmed in America are generally all right, but the giant ones from the Atlantic are fished with bad gear. Crustaceans like lobster and crab weren't depleted at press time because the predators that feed on them are overfished, but as with all seafood, keep an eye out for where they come from. For farmed fish, barramundi is a current eco-darling, as it's raised in land-based closed containment systems that don't pollute. It gets high marks from the Blue Ocean Institute and the Marine Stewardship Council. But Environmental Defense says to avoid non-U.S.-farmed barramundi.

SEE SHELLS? EAT THEM.

Some seafood experts estimate that 90 percent of big ocean fish have been eaten, and they project a global collapse of fisheries by 2048. Clearly, making sustainable dinner choices is crucial. As it turns out, some crustaceans—lobsters, oysters, scallops, clams, mussels, abalone, et cetera—can be quite sustainable, not to mention safe to eat, even when farmed. An unexpected bonus: Most bivalves are filter feeders, so they act as water filters of sorts, improving water quality. Check out your favorite crustacean on a seafood guide before shopping; each species has its own environmental and health concerns, depending on the waters and countries it's from.

LITTLE SHRIMP, BIG IMPACT

If you, like many Americans, eat shrimp often, there are a few things you should know. Most wild shrimp are caught in polluted waters with destructive trawlers. Farmed tend to be fed bad feed (though there are some people farming them ecologically). A text to FishPhone reveals that U.S. and Canadian northern, pink, or farmed shrimp have very few environmental concerns, Gulf of Mexico shrimp have some environmental concerns, and imported shrimp should be avoided because they have significant environmental concerns. Unfortunately, the best shrimp are hard to locate in stores. In his book *Bottomfeeder*, Taras Grescoe details other concerns: "If the shrimp in your supermarket display case glisten unnaturally, or if they taste soapy even after being cooked, they have probably been treated with STPP, or sodium tripolyphosphate, the suspected neurotoxicant used to prevent drying . . . A grainy substance coating the shell could mean the shrimp has been treated with caustic borax, to prevent discoloration." Yuck.

MICHAEL POLLAN'S SALMON WRAPPED IN FIG LEAVES WITH KALE, INSPIRED BY CHEZ PANISSE

Pollan buys his salmon in Berkeley, California, at Monterey Fish Market on Hopkins Street, and suggests using wild Alaskan salmon or Loch Duart for farmed. For the fig leaves, "If you don't have a fig tree and don't live in a place where they grow outdoors, go to a nursery and 'prune' a couple," says Pollan. Preferably unsprayed!

Serves 4

4 pieces (3 to 4 ounces each) boneless, skinless salmon
Olive oil
Coarse salt and freshly ground pepper
4 fig leaves
1/2 pound kale, torn into small pieces

1. Preheat the oven to 350°F.

2. Drizzle the salmon with olive oil and season with salt and pepper. Wrap each piece of salmon in a fig leaf and place it on a baking sheet. Transfer to the oven and bake until the fish is cooked through, 10 to 12 minutes.

3. Meanwhile, place kale on a baking sheet. Pour the olive oil into a spray bottle. Spray the kale with olive oil and season with salt and pepper. Transfer to the oven and bake until the kale is crispy, about 8 minutes.

4. Unwrap the salmon and serve immediately on fig leaves with the kale.

SURFING FOR SEAFOOD

If you don't have access to a good fish market, or your local fish are impossibly polluted, ordering sustainable fish online may be for you. Some locavores won't even consider flying in safe fish for dinner, but Blue Hill chef Dan Barber feels that buying from a well-regulated fishery is important to the ecosystem, particularly of the Pacific Northwest, and is "worth the environmental degradation of flying something across the country." He doesn't do it often—wild salmon and the like are on his New York menus infrequently—and admits, "This is a purely personal calculation. I can understand people who say it's not worth it. In this particular case, I feel completely invested in supporting a fishery that's a good example of what a fishery should be, going into the future. They have regulation during the catch and holistic management in place." *Real Food* author Nina Planck suggests the "frozen at

---

FURTHER READING

If you want to dive even deeper into this arena, here are a few must-read books, plus websites to bookmark:

- *What to Eat: An Aisle-by-Aisle Guide to Savvy Food Choices and Good Eating* by Marion Nestle
- *Bottomfeeder: How to Eat Ethically in a World of Vanishing Seafood* by Taras Grescoe
- *Diagnosis: Mercury: Money, Politics, and Poison* by Jane M. Hightower, M.D.
- Daniel Pauly, fisheries scientist at the University of British Columbia: Fisheries.UBC.ca/members/dpauly
- FishBase.org

---

sea" Alaskan salmon from Vital Choice (VitalChoice.com) on her website, and also gives a nod to troll-caught albacore tuna (AlbaTuna.com).

ACT UP!

It's unconscionable that it's up to consumers to do this much work to eat the safest possible fish. If you agree, it's time to get political. Join forces with environmental groups (see "Online Guides," page 89) and tell the powers that be that you want stronger regulation, better labeling, cleaner waterways, and safer, sustainable fish.

CHAPTER SIX

drinks

LITTLE THINGS ADD UP, INCLUDING THE THINGS WE DRINK every day—sometimes several times a day—like coffee and wine. These universal beverages present an easy opportunity to make a difference without much effort. This doesn't require living across the street from a natural spring or a café that stocks the finest fairtrade, locally roasted brew around (though if you've got that, by all means). The first step is to consider them at all—it's amazing how many dedicated organophiles I meet who have never thought about what's in the cup they're drinking from. It's as if we've all been programmed to consider fruit, veggies, meat, and fish, but forget about the liquids we imbibe. Herewith, some information to help deprogram—then reprogram—you. Thirsty? Let's start with H_2O.

WATER

Fresh from the chapter on fish, you already know that our waterways are polluted. Despite this contamination, choosing to drink bottled water over municipal water is not the answer. The Environmental Protection Agency's standards for tap water are actually higher and more enforceable than the Food and Drug Administration's for bottled water (oddly, the two are not regulated by the same agency). Multiple studies have now proven that bottled water is actually often less regulated and more contaminated than the municipal water— aka tap water—that most people are seeking to avoid when they go for bottled. I repeat: Tap water is held to higher standards and is more regulated than bottled. This isn't disputed, even by the Government Accountability Office, the congressional overseer (GAO.gov). The Environmental Working Group (EWG), a nonprofit public health and environment watchdog/advocacy group that conducts consumer-friendly and very educational studies (many of them referenced throughout these pages), came out with one such water study in 2008. It revealed that bottled water contained disinfection by-products, fertilizer residue, and pain medication. These things may also be in some tap water, and clearly tap has issues, some more than others, but at least with tap you haven't paid for and been involved with the transportation of something you believed to be free of these very substances.

Some other interesting tidbits from the EWG report (EWG.org):

- Citizens are provided with local tap water test results yearly, but the bottled water industry doesn't publicly disclose the results of any contaminant testing that it conducts.
- Bottled water costs consumers 1,900 times as much as tap water.
- Consumers are led to believe bottled is purer than tap, but tests conducted for EWG found that ten popular brands of bottled water, purchased from grocery stores across the country, contained thirty-eight chemical pollutants altogether, with an average of eight contaminants in each brand. Levels of these same pollutants and contaminants in tap water vary by municipality.

"More than one-third of the chemicals found are not regulated in bottled water," states the report. ". . . Our tests strongly indicate that the purity of bottled water cannot be trusted. Given the industry's refusal to make available data to support their claims of superiority, consumer confidence in the purity of bottled water is simply not justified."

Besides bottled water being an overpriced rip-off, the environmental impact of all of those petrochemical-derived plastic bottles is huge. Curbside plastic collection programs appear to have given consumers the false feeling that plastic can be environmentally friendly, making people comfortable buying more of it. But the resulting increase in use means that the overall amount of plastic being sent to landfills isn't actually going down—despite recycling—according to the Berkeley, California–based Ecology Center (Ecology Center.org). The Government Accountability Office says that 75 percent of water bottles are just thrown in the trash. Of the bottles that are recycled, some are eventually made into secondary products that aren't recyclable, like textiles or plastic lumber. More from the Ecology Center: "Plastic packaging has economic, health, and environmental costs and benefits. While offering advantages such as flexibility and light weight, it creates problems including: consumption of fossil resources; pollution; high energy use in manufacturing; accumulation of wasted plastic in the environment; and migration of polymers and additives into foods." Although the plastic that most water bottles are made of (PET#1) has long been considered okay healthwise, reports are starting to surface that it leaches hormone-disrupting phthalates (see page 155 for more on plastics).

Not enough to make you give up plastic water bottles? Search

tip

Seltzer and club soda are bottled water, too. If you like fizz in your H_2O, either locate a local seltzer home delivery service or buy a home soda maker and create it yourself. Be sure to use only glass or stainless-steel canisters, not plastic. SodaStream makes a glass version that doesn't require batteries or electricity to turn tap into sparkling water: SodaStreamUSA.com.

the Internet for images of the masses of plastic that are floating in the middle of the ocean (try Googling Great Pacific Garbage Patch), or look at how many you see littered all over the streets on your next walk. Speaking of litter, a PET bottle in a landfill will take more than one thousand years to biodegrade. The numbers change yearly, but not too long ago, the Container Recycling Institute (Container-Recycling .org) estimated that forty million plastic water bottles a day are tossed in landfills. And we haven't even scratched the surface of the plastic water bottle problem when you consider that millions of barrels of oil are used each year to produce them.

Yes, certain bottled water companies have launched campaigns to prove that they're not so bad (some even claim to be "green"), including initiatives to reduce the weight of their plastic bottles and cut transportation emissions. But bottled water is frivolous in any place in the world that has adequate drinking water. It boggles the mind that the bottled water business is booming despite the fact that it's indisputably environmentally

tip

Don't reuse plastic #1 water bottles by refilling them in an effort to go green. They are not meant for more than one use. They're tough to clean, harbor bacteria, and can break down over time— especially in sunlight (like when sitting on a car dashboard) or in heat (like when washed in a dishwasher)—and release their chemical components into your beverage.

THE LIST: WATER
A sliding scale of choices from best to worst

• Tested and filtered tap water in a glass (at home) or a nonplastic reusable water bottle (on the go)

AVOID: Bottled water

unfriendly, no healthier than most U.S. tap water, and it's wildly overpriced. Stop the madness.

Testing Water

Municipal water, unlike bottled water, is tested and regulated. The results are public information. If you're curious about what yours might contain, as you should be, ask your water utility company for a copy of the annual water quality report. Even if your municipal water is good, you still might want to test what flows out of your tap if you live in an older building or house. This will show you what might be coming out of your pipes—like lead—into your water. Plumbing installed before 1930 tends to contain lead pipes, and lead solder is still used on newer copper pipes. Old pipes don't automatically equal contaminated water; years of mineral deposits from water can coat the walls of lead pipes, creating a barrier of sorts.

In New York, where I live, the city tests tap water for free— just call 311 and they'll send you the kits. Check with your municipal government to see if they also test for free in your hometown. If

---

REUSABLE WATER BOTTLES

If canvas bags are the new plastic bag, surely the reusable water bottle is the new plastic water bottle. In this arena, I avoid the plastic reusable water bottles altogether, even the BPA-free ones, and drink out of metal versions—stainless steel is preferable to aluminum. Go shopping. Kleen Kanteen (KleenKanteen.com) is one stainless-steel brand. There are many others. If you find a brand that lines the interior of the bottle with something, make sure you know exactly what it is, or don't buy it. Or reuse a glass juice bottle. Or fill up a glass Ball jar. Then tuck it in your nonplastic bag and go.

CHOOSING A FILTER

According to the Natural Resources Defense Council, all filters used should adhere to the joint National Sanitation Foundation (NSF.org) and American National Standards Institute (ANSI.org) Standard 53, which covers drinking-water treatment units. This isn't a 100 percent guarantee of safety, but at least NSF-certified filters have been independently tested to show that they can, in fact, reduce levels of certain pollutants under specified conditions. If you're comparing and contrasting filters, the NRDC maintains a helpful Consumer Guide to Water Filters at NRDC.org/water/drinking/gfilters.asp. *Consumer Reports* (GreenerChoices.org) has also rated filters in the past.

not, call your local department of health services for testing advice, or find out where water can be tested by visiting the Environmental Protection Agency's Safe Water site—EPA.gov/SafeWater. If your water has a problem, the testing agency will advise on how best to fix it.

After testing, all most tap water needs—unless there is an issue—is an activated carbon filter, such as Brita. The websites for various filters will say what substances they reduce. These usually include chlorine, lead, copper, cadmium, mercury, arsenic, and benzene, as well as some parasites like giardia, plus odors and "bad" flavor. Even though everything tested within allowable levels in my water at home, I personally still use a filter to further reduce whatever levels I have of the above, and to protect myself against what might arise in the reservoir or corrode in my pipes over time. There are bogus filtering products on the market, so

tip

Not all filters are recyclable. Double-check before buying to see if yours is. Both Zero Water (ZeroWater.com) and Brita (Brita.com, in a partnership with Preserve: Preserve Products.com) currently recycle.

buy only certified filters—see "Choosing a Filter," page 101). And do your research before choosing a filter. In 2009, the Center for Environmental Health (CEH.org) filed complaints in California Superior Court against the manufacturers, distributors, and sellers of certain activated carbon filters, claiming they actually release arsenic into water and that the defendants, including Multi-Pure International; Omnipure Filter Co., Inc.; PUR Water Purification Products, Inc.; the Proctor & Gamble Co.; General Electric Company; Cuno Incorporated; Ecowater Systems, LLC; Everpure, LLC; K.X. Industries, L.P.; Sears, Roebuck and Co.; and Whirlpool Water Products knew or should have known that, and should have warned consumers. Check CEH's site for the most recent information.

Well Water

If your source of water is a well, local agriculture extension services can help you locate well water testers near you. The Environmental Protection Agency's ground water and drinking water site (EPA .gov/SafeWater) includes links to connect private well owners to state-by-state guidance and information. Issues with well water are usually bacteria and nitrates, plus radon, lead, atrazine (see page 25) and other pesticides, radium, and volatile organic compounds, not to mention taste and odor problems. Filtration systems for well

TRYING TO AVOID PLASTIC?

Most activated carbon filter pitchers are made of plastic. Until someone makes a glass or stainless-steel pitcher, plastic-avoiders (see page 154) can rely on faucet-mount filters, or transfer their water, once filtered, into a glass carafe. If you have an in-fridge water filtration system, use it. Just double-check that it meets NSF/ANSI standards (see page 101).

DRUGGY WATERS

Studies have shown that pharmaceuticals and other personal care products—like hormone-disrupting residues from lotions, perfumes, and cosmetics—are present in some of our waterways. Scientists are busily studying the ecological impact of those residues as well as their effects on human health. Some water filter companies now claim that their products reduce the levels of these drugs in drinking water, but I'm not yet convinced that this is possible to do on any real scale. The best we can all do to help the situation involves two things:

1. Use only certified natural cosmetics and/or those made with organic ingredients that do not contain hormone disrupters and other harsh chemicals that will wind up in our water.

2. Dispose of all pharmaceuticals properly by following the White House Office of National Drug Control Policy's disposal of prescription drugs guidelines: Go to WhiteHouseDrugPolicy.gov and search for "proper disposal."

water, if a problem is found, can be more extensive than your average activated carbon carafe.

OTHER BEVERAGES

Sodas, diet sodas, vitamin waters, and all sorts of sugar/corn syrup/ fake sugar–infused drinks don't really have a place in a conscious kitchen. If you're interested in drinking them, that's your prerogative. Read the labels, make smart decisions, and limit your intake. And don't forget, they usually come in the very same plastic that bottled water comes in, or in BPA-lined

tip

Dying for a soda? Buy a seltzer maker. Make seltzer. Add real fruit juice. Delicious!

aluminum cans. So the health and environmental impacts are well known.

JUICE

Fresh squeezed, 100 percent juice is fabulous in moderation. Thankfully it's so expensive at my local organic juice bar that moderation isn't a problem. If you're someone who really likes juice, look into buying an energy-efficient juicer. Having your own means you can control what kind of fruit is used (local or organic or sustainable), how much and what kind of sugar is added, and how the machine is cleaned.

Alternatives to fresh squeezed are a mixed bag. Most storebought juice actually contains very little juice, so it's up to an adept

---

THE IMPACT OF YOUR DAILY OJ

In 2009 PepsiCo, which owns Tropicana, hired experts to figure out the overall energy footprint of their orange juice. Emissions from running a factory and transporting the heavy cartons were taken into account, but when all numbers were crunched, the worst emission-making culprit in the orange-grove-to-consumer production line turned out to be (drum roll, please) growing oranges conventionally. From a *New York Times* article on the study: "Citrus groves use a lot of nitrogen fertilizer, which requires natural gas to make and can turn into a potent greenhouse gas when it is spread on fields." Replacing your OJ with an organic version, or even home-made juice, are better options if you live near organic citrus groves, though slightly less so if you don't. Other comparisons have shown that there's more packaging waste in shipping whole oranges than in shipping the juice itself. Sadly, oranges don't grow in my area. Apples do, and who doesn't love apple cider? I treat fresh-squeezed orange juice like a luxury. I don't drink it daily. But on the rare occasions I do—heaven.

---

label reader to find the real deal. Otherwise, you may suck down a lot of unnecessary and expensive sugar water (along with other unexpected additives, like synthetic fragrance). Organic jarred or cartoned juices are sometimes guilty of containing as much sugar or sweeteners as their conventional counterparts, but at least it's not derived from genetically modified corn (see page 130). When it comes to artificial sweeteners, all bets are off. I don't put those things in my body, and suggest you don't either. Real sugar is vastly preferable, unless, of course, you have a medical condition that means you can't tolerate it.

COFFEE

Chances are you, dear reader living in the United States, don't live near a coffee plantation. For all of this talk about eating locally, coffee rarely falls under that rubric. It's truly a global product. Locavores who follow a very strict one-hundred-ish-mile diet may therefore opt to give it up entirely, while others choose to keep drinking coffee as one of their grandfathered-in non-local items. Those of us still hopped-up on the mighty beans (me included) like to point out that if everyone who didn't live near coffee stopped drinking it, the farmers who grow it would be in trouble. The key thing with coffee is to source it carefully, especially since by some estimates it is the second most widely traded global commodity after oil. Think of the eco-repercussions of drinking the worst-farmed beans, 365 days a year. When it comes to coffee, the best brew goes beyond just choosing organic or sustainable beans

tip The most energy-efficient gadgets to go with your eco-friendly **beans** include hand-crank grinders and glass and stainless-steel French presses over their plastic, electricity-using counterparts.

for personal and environmental health. Here are a couple of additional issues:

Workers' Wages and Treatment

Coffee is, for the most part, grown in poor and/or developing countries, to be drunk, for the most part, by people with more money in richer countries. Stateside, it's cheap. A cup at a café costs only a buck or two, so you can imagine how little the farmers growing it are actually making. To ensure that the workers growing your coffee are being treated right, look for fair-trade certification (TransFairUSA.org) on your bag of beans. This, they say, takes into account fair prices, labor conditions, direct trade, democratic and transparent organizations, community development, as well as environmental sustainability—the last of which is especially crucial for the rain forests, where a great deal of coffee is grown. Fair Trade Certified products tend to come from small producers on small farms that belong to larger cooperatives.

tip

Most decaf coffees are made by soaking beans in solvents. The most toxic—like benzene—are now banned, but methylene chloride, a paint stripper, is still in use. Look for CO_2 or water (aka Swiss Water Method) processed decaf instead. Do the research before you shop; it's the rare bag of decaf that spells out how it was processed.

Birds/Natural Habitat

Coffee traditionally grows in the shade, under a natural canopy that's home to many birds. According to *Sierra* magazine (Sierra Club.org/Sierra), low-quality coffee can be grown more easily and cheaply in full sun, "but only with extensive use of pesticides." Cutting down the canopy is not only eco-destructive but eliminates bird habitat. To avoid further destruction, look for labels like "Shade Grown" and "Bird Friendly" (ShadeCoffee.org) when shopping. The Rainforest Alliance certification label covers both worker treatment and birds (Rainforest-Alliance.org).

· · ·

The differences between fair-trade and Rainforest Alliance certifications are subtle, but the going thought is that TransFair USA advocates more strongly for workers (they offer a price guarantee) as well as the environment. Rainforest Alliance certification tends to be found on larger-scale coffee operations than those certified as fair trade. Coffee and fair-trade fanatics can compare and contrast these certifications at length, but keep in mind that choosing either over conventional coffee is key. Responsibly grown coffee tastes as good as its conventional counterpart— and I'd argue a lot better—without a huge added expense. The price might seem different if what you're used to is the cheapest canned coffee available. But if you're already paying for expensive brand-name grounds, pods, or beans, switching to conscious coffee won't hurt your wallet, and will help farmers and the earth. If you aren't prepared to make the switch, at the very least try to avoid coffee made by the biggest companies, which are Kraft, Nestlé, Sara Lee, and Procter & Gamble, according to Treehugger.com. From the site: "These coffee biggies helped engineer a huge overproduction of coffee that made coffee farmers dirt poor—a situation dubbed the coffee crisis. The four also got the American public used to drinking swill. If you're drinking canned Folgers coffee, you're probably downing twigs, dust, and floor sweepings."

tip

Fair-trade certification goes beyond coffee. Look for the label on other exotics like tea, chocolate, vanilla, fruit (including bananas), rice, sugar, and flowers.

tip

Don't like what's on offer at the office? Bring your home brew in a thermos, or French press it at your desk.

BEYOND BEANS:
GREENING THE COFFEE-DRINKING EXPERIENCE

It's environmentally preferable to make your coffee at home. There you choose the milk, the paper-packet-free fair-trade sugar (page 128), the filters (reusable or at least unbleached paper). Other things to try: Avoid paper pods, drink out of a mug, and compost the grounds. Take a mug with you to work, too, and talk to whoever does the buying about getting organic and Fair Trade Certified goods and better milk.

tip

You're most likely to find eco-responsible brew at small independent cafés. They depend on their clientele, so if they're not pouring what you want to be drinking, ask them to. They might be happy to accommodate a good customer. For eco-leaning cafés listed by state, check out DineGreen.com or TransFairUSA.org.

When out and about, take a mug—or a travel cup or thermos, preferably not plastic—with you, or at the very least ask your favorite barista to stock compostable cups. See if you can inspire them to give their grounds to a local composting group.

THE LIST: COFFEE AND TEA
A sliding scale of choices from best to worst

- Fair Trade Certified and organic, or Fair Trade Certified and sustainable, plus Bird Friendly
- Rainforest Alliance Certified and organic or Rainforest Alliance Certified and sustainable
- Organic or sustainable

AVOID: Conventional coffee and teas, especially those produced by the biggest companies

SOME SOURCES FOR COFFEE AND TEA

CafeAltaGracia.com

InPursuitOfTea.com

IrvingFarm.com

JacksStirBrew.com

Sacred-Grounds.com

SamovarLife.com

SweetMarias.com

VermontCoffeeCompany.com

TEA

Tea is said to be the world's most-consumed beverage, excluding water. This doesn't appear to be true in the United States, but it's undeniable that in recent years, even here in the United States, certain teas from specific estates have taken on a sort of cult-like following. These small farm teas are often hand produced, meant to be brewed with precision, and pricey. However you like your tea, the issues to consider are similar to those with coffee. From white to fermented pu-erh to oolong, tea can be heavily sprayed, so organic is preferable. And Fair Trade Certified is a must.

tip To avoid extraneous packaging, buy loose-leaf teas and steep in reusable strainers.

ORGANIC VS. SUSTAINABLE CUPPA

Within the wide world of tea, there is a lively organic versus uncertified small farm debate that mirrors the organic versus local produce debate (see page 28). It's one you'll have to decide for yourself if you drink a lot of tea, and you'll likely mix and match, unless you're always drinking high-end tea. Sebastian Beckwith, founder of the well-regarded company In Pursuit of Tea, meticulously curates and sells small farm teas grown using age-old

DIY HERBAL

Herbal infusions can be as local as your yard, garden, or even your window box. Make sure you use organic soil, then plant anything you like to drink. Just double-check that what you plant is safe to infuse. Then put on the kettle, snip, steep, and sip. In the summer, pour these concoctions over ice. Chef Daniel Sauer of the Outermost Inn in Martha's Vineyard makes an herbal tea with a base of mint. "I use three different kinds: blackmint, peppermint, and spearmint, then add whatever I can find—lemon balm, lemon verbena. The only herb to watch out for is lemon thyme—too much can turn the tea bitter."

sustainable and chemical-free techniques. They're not certified organic. He says his teas taste better and are of better quality than machine processed teas. Worth a sip.

HEY EARL GREY FANS:

Did you know that the bergamot flavoring used to give it that signature taste is almost always synthetic? Choose organic tea to avoid artificial flavoring.

WINE

Conventional grapes are an intensely sprayed crop. But somehow even people who eat organic food neglect to drink organic wine. It may be an oversight, or maybe it's because organic wine has long had a stigma of not being too tasty. Luckily this reputation is now undeserved. If you stop to think about the sprays, and about how, exactly, those inexpensive Australian/Chilean/Italian bottles get all the way to your doorstep, you might find yourself looking for something organic and slightly more local, maybe even from a vineyard you can visit. Finding a good organic local wine has been a tall order for me personally, as the wine-growing regions closest to me do not, for the most part, produce many organic grapes (see "A Fruity Situation" page 43) or the most delicious wines. My current very local and delicious Long Island gems come from the sustainably managed Shinn Estate Vineyard (ShinnVineyard .RecipesFromHome.com).

Organic Grape Options

Certified organic wines are few and far between because organic standards do not permit the use of sulfites, the bacteria-killing preservatives used in making pretty much all wine. Some producers use organic grapes and add varying degrees of sulfites, resulting in wine that cannot technically be certified organic. These wines are often labeled "made with organically grown grapes" and are a good option. Unfortunately, not all winemakers using organic grapes choose to call this out on their labels. This is a shame. If you're growing organically, you should shout it from the rooftops to make it easy for consumers to find.

"Biodynamic" is a third-party-certified method and term (Demeter-USA.org) that's a bit confusing to explain. Basically biodynamic farming shares many tenets with organic farming (no synthetic pesticides or fertilizers are permitted—some people call it a forerunner to the organic movement) but takes it several steps further. Biodynamic vineyards have not only vines but also other plants, trees, and animals, all of which work together as a unified system—this is called biodiversity. It also involves sowing and planting according to the cycle of the moon, and all farming practices are done with reverence for the land. Since Rudolf Steiner

THE LIST: WINE AND GRAPES
A sliding scale of options from best to worst

- Biodynamic
- Certified organic. (Certified wines from other countries will be labeled with foreign versions of the USDA organic stamp like Ecocert or Australian Certified Organic.)
- Wines labeled "organically grown" or "made with organically grown grapes"
- Bottles marked "sustainably grown" or "made with sustainably grown grapes"

AVOID: Wine made with conventionally grown grapes

helped establish the principles of biodynamic farming in 1924, and it involves some metaphysical practices, some people dismiss these methods as overly spiritual, or out there, like yoga was regarded before it became chic. How shortsighted to dismiss something so lovely. My layperson's take is that biodynamic farmers are land whisperers. I'm delighted to have people obsessed with the health of their soil, vines, and animals make my wine, and feel very safe sipping (or eating) anything grown biodynamically.

Truly Natural Wine

Jenny & François Selections (WorldWideWine.net) imports natural French wines. In the world of food labeling, "natural" isn't particularly meaningful, but after speaking with cofounder Jenny Lefcourt, I came to understand that the natural wine movement is very specific and meaningful. Lefcourt's small vineyard winemakers go well beyond organic and sometimes even beyond biodynamic. It's a unique list, arguably the purest of what I've tasted.

Natural winemakers try to avoid additives as much as possible, and certainly never use anything synthetic. Sulfites are the additives that most wine drinkers are aware of (they're the only one listed on bottles), but there are actually two hundred additives that can be used in wine. Many conventional winemakers use lab-produced yeasts to aid fermentation because their overuse of sulfites kills off not only bacteria but also natural yeast. They also rely on additives like sugars and acids to adjust the flavor of grapes that don't taste like they're supposed to anymore, thanks to years of pesticide use. Natural winemakers grow their vines in healthier, spray-free soil and therefore have healthier grapes that require fewer additives, and less of any one. "Natural is about making quality choices, lowering yields, and hand picking in small containers instead of machine harvest," says Lefcourt. She and her partner import to many states, from Oregon to North Dakota to Kentucky. I have tasted most of what they bring to New York—and even visited one of their winemakers in France—and the wines are quite a bit different from what I'm used to. They are

---

OTHER STAMPS

There are other less common eco-labels you may come across on bottles of American wine: LiveInc.org, found mainly in Oregon and Washington, is based on a third-party-verified checklist system and signifies that the vineyard uses native insects and pest-deterring plants as a way to reduce the use of chemical pesticides. Salmon Safe (SalmonSafe.org) is also a Northwestern thing, and the certification means that farmers have taken steps—beyond using natural pest control and including planting trees and growing cover crops—not to harm salmon habitats via runoff in the process of producing wine. SIP (Sustainability in Practice) certified is a nationwide seal that verifies how the fruit was grown. SIP wines must contain 85 percent SIP certified fruit (SipTheGoodLife.org).

---

for the most part very much alive—over the course of drinking a bottle they open up and taste surprisingly different. Our (current) house red is a Jenny & François selection, Chateau Haut Lavigne Cotes de Duras 2006. I was amused to realize our winemaker, like our CSA farmer, is a woman: Nadia Lusseau. Bonus: It's about twelve dollars a bottle. Natural (or organic or biodynamic or sustainable) wine doesn't necessarily mean more expensive.

Wine Miles

Considering how far wine—organic, biodynamic, or otherwise— must travel to most of us, it's only natural that people have attempted to calculate wine's carbon footprint. This is a too-complicated-for-words math problem that takes into account growing, making, transporting, and everything in between. In general, these carbon comparisons are thought provoking, but they're not the only way to determine what to drink. One must-read is "Red, White and 'Green': The Cost of Carbon in the Global Wine Trade," by Tyler Colman (aka the wine blogger Dr. Vino) and Pablo Päster (who holds the fabulous title "sustainability metrics specialist"), a paper written for the American Association of Wine Economists. Their findings show that while organic farming

---

WATER WORKS

If the ins and outs of organic/biodynamic/natural wines are of interest, another interesting topic is irrigation. In most places, including the United States, vineyards are irrigated, which makes for higher yields and alcohol levels. This practice is illegal in much of Europe, most notably in France, mainly because of established traditions, and a fear that it will alter taste. An environmental advantage of this tradition is that it saves water, a scarce commodity in many places where wine is grown. For the skinny on irrigation (and more), read *The Battle for Wine and Love* by Alice Feiring.

FINDING CONSCIOUS (AND TASTY) WINE

To find the greenest wines, shop independent stores over supermarkets. The person doing the selections can guide you. The following questions will lead you to the purest bottles in any store:

- Do you have any certified organic or certified biodynamic wines? Do you carry anything made with organically grown grapes?
- Do you carry any naturally made artisanal wines? Are they hand-picked or fermented with indigenous (not lab) yeast?

This inexhaustive list of importers (contact them to see where their selections are sold), wine journals, and a few retailers will lead you to conscious wine wherever you live.

Natural

- JonDavidWine.com
- KermitLynch.com
- LeSerbet.com
- LouisDressner.com
- MadRose.com
- SkurnikWines.com/Terry_Theise
- WorldWideWine.net

Organic and Biodynamic

- AppellationNYC.com
- ForkandBottle.com/wine/biodynamic_producers.htm
- OrganicWineJournal.com
- RedWhiteandGreen.com.au
- SkurnikWines.com and click on Our Organic Wineries

has lower total greenhouse-gas output, transportation plays a more significant role in the overall wine footprint, and distance matters. They conclude: "Efficiencies in transportation make container ships better than trucks, which in turn are better than planes." Bigger bottles (magnums) are more carbon-friendly, since the glass-to-wine ratio is less. Light packing materials have less carbon intensity. These include Tetra Pak (what kids' juice boxes are made of) or boxes lined in plastic bags. This is a carbon footprint paper, so there's no mention here that drinking out of plastic raises potential health concerns. Also, "Shipping wine in bulk from the source and bottling closer to the point of consumption lowers carbon intensity."

The biggest tip to take away from this study is the authors' contention that for U.S. wine drinkers, there's a "green line" that runs down the middle of Ohio. "For points to the west of that line, it is more carbon efficient to consume wine trucked from California. To the east of that line, it's more efficient to consume the same-sized bottle of wine from Bordeaux, which has benefited from the efficiencies of container shipping, followed by a shorter truck trip." I'm not sure how you know if something was shipped versus flown. Apparently French wine is in general shipped via boat, which pollutes less than trucking it from California to the East Coast. We need better labeling to reduce this guesswork for consumers, but for now, I'm trying to favor French on my side of the green line, when not drinking local.

THE HARD STUFF

There are equally interesting organic—and sometimes even handmade—vodkas, gins, tequilas, and other spirits on the market. Local is tough to find in the hard liquor arena, but it's not impossible, especially if you happen to live in bourbon country. The following libations might not be available at your local watering hole yet, but are worthy of a spot in your home bar. To name a few organic vodkas: Sunshine (made with 100 percent certified organic grain and Vermont spring water); Square One (distilled with certified organic American rye and water from "deep Wyoming aquifers"); Prairie (made in Minnesota from local certified organic corn); Tru (made from organic American wheat and by a company that says they're carbon negative); and Rain (made from single farm organic

Illinois corn, and distilled in Kentucky). Even beverage giant Anheuser-Busch makes a vodka from 100 percent organic Italian wheat and wrapped in "tree-free" paper with soy-based inks—it's called Purus. Some of these vodkas come flavored with certified organic lemons, cucumbers, and more. Some don't. If you're mixing, pour with organic tonic.

There's slightly less variety for other liquors. Tru also makes an organic gin, as does Juniper Green. The best-known organic tequila may be 4 Copas. Cuca Fresca is a "green" Brazilian rum, and Papagayo organic rums come spiced or white all the way from Paraguay. There's also an organic (and strong tasting) acai spirit called VeeV, a Brazilian cachaça called Leblon, and a limoncello-style line of organic liqueurs called Loft. These come in ginger, lavender, and (biodynamically grown) lemongrass. Want a cognac? Pour Délice d'Orange Roland Seguin's versions, infused with organic fruit. Single malt Scotch whiskey fans aren't left high and dry—they can sip Benromach Organic Speyside. Another treat—the handcrafted whiskeys and more from Tuthilltown Spirits in upstate New York, made from local corn, rye, potatoes, and apples. Everything you'd need for a seriously organic party. Enjoy.

BEER

Because the various ingredients that go into beer come from many different places, it reminds me more of packaged food than of wine. Consider ingredient sourcing, water usage, bottling, and transportation issues, and sipping a cold one becomes less relaxing than it should be.

To find the best-choice brew, start with organic: buying organic beer—especially from makers that aren't the biggest beer companies—is a great idea. The dream, as with everything from cheese to cucumbers, is to buy both organic and local. And here we hit a roadblock. Even if you could find beer's ingredients— water, yeast, malt, and hops—in your area (and that's a huge if), it doesn't mean they're processed locally. In fact, according to Max Oswald, director of sales and marketing at the Otter Creek Brewing Company in Middlebury, Vermont, the grain used for the malt in their Wolaver's organic beer must be shipped to the Midwest to be processed. Why? Because that is where malt processing is done in

tip

For further conscious beer reading: *Fermenting Revolution: How to Drink Beer and Save the World* by Christopher Mark O'Brien; BrewOrganic.com; and GreenGrog.com.

FIND ORGANIC BEER NEAR YOU

Many small organic breweries serve only their surrounding area, so ask around. If you're invested in supporting independent breweries, double-check to see that the organic beer you're interested in isn't made by a Big Beer company; this is not always apparent on the label. Also, many companies that make organic beers—including some of the breweries listed below—also make conventional beers, so make sure you're buying the one you want. This is by no means a complete list:

- California: EelRiverBrewing.com; BisonBrew.com
- Colorado: NewBelgium.com
- Maine: PeakBrewing.com
- Maryland: CCBeer.com/beerlist/Oxford+Organic+Ales
- North Carolina: PisgahBrewing.com
- Oregon: HopWorksBeer.com
- Vermont: OtterCreekBrewing.com/wolavers.html; ecobrew.net
- Wisconsin: LakeFrontBrewery.com/organic_esb.html
- Wyoming: SnakeRiverBrewing.com

this country. "It's a conundrum. We do the best we can," says Oswald.

Hops

A real issue with organic beer is hops, the bitter flowers of a climbing vine that serve to both counterbalance sweet malt and preserve beer. Oswald refers to hops as "kind of like seasoning, like oregano in tomato sauce." It's a pest-prone crop that's difficult to grow, and very difficult to grow organically.

Organic hops tend to be grown in the Pacific Northwest, Europe, and New Zealand. Vermont-based Wolaver's uses New Zealand organic hops and works with a contract grower in Oregon. The goal is to rely solely on Oregon. This is as local as it will get. The Northeast used to produce tons of hops, but the crops were wiped out by fungus. Other organic brewers are also taking this route of contracting small organic farmers. Meanwhile, the USDA, in response to a hops shortage in 2008, has put hops on their exemption list, meaning beer made with nonorganic hops but that is otherwise organic can still be labeled USDA organic—music to Big Beer's ears, and not exactly motivating to any farmers attempting to grow the vines the way they should be grown. (The amount of hops in any beer, it should be noted, is pretty minimal. But still.)

At the Brewery

Though it is difficult for any brewer to source all-organic, all-local ingredients, there are other environmentally friendly steps they can take with their brewery. Otter Creek, according to Oswald, has redone their lighting, runs a boiler system on biodiesel, tries to reuse heat and water, and recycles their grain by giving it to farmers for feed. "We have a wastewater pretreatment system inside the plant so we don't send any effluent into the municipal sewer system, and we're working to be able to utilize our spent grain for fuel,"

BOTTLES VS. CANS, PLUS PACKAGING

What's better to drink out of, a glass bottle or a can? Glass, please. It's better for the earth (aluminum mining is destructive) and easier to recycle, not to mention that the hormone-disrupting chemical BPA is found in cans (see page 155). An extra tip: Choose glass bottled without paper labels. These are just more waste, even if they're fun to peel as you drink. Also, check out what the case boxes are made of, as some companies use recycled content cardboard over new bleached material. If these contain beer you like to drink, choose them.

says Oswald. This is an expensive and lofty goal for the smallish brewery—in 2008 they were doing about thirty-three thousand barrels, one-third of which was organic—but it will make quite a difference. Many other breweries are also working to reduce their energy consumption. Some have green roofs, others are using solar power. Still others make sure their used equipment is made only in the United States.

CHAPTER SEVEN

packaged foods

PROCESSED PACKAGED FOODS HAVE NO PLACE IN A WHOLE foods diet. Everyone is better off without products made with multiple ingredients sourced from all over the world, processed at far-flung factories into something new (Corn-syrup-sweetened cookie that may contain mercury? Energy bar containing peanut butter that gets recalled for salmonella?), packaged within an inch of its life (perhaps wrapped in something that contains chemicals you don't want touching your food, and that you won't be able to recycle), and then transported in chilled trucks, boats, or airplanes. It's common sense that it's healthier to make these things yourself (or approximations thereof) than to buy out of the frozen foods section, even if it's USDA certified organic. (Organic junk food is still junk food! Plus, multi-ingredient products with the USDA organic seal are only required to be 95 percent organic, though some are 100 percent.) Otherwise, there's too much unknown—about where the various food components came from, about the carbon footprint, about how many people or machines touched the food before you bought it. And beyond the food miles and food safety issues, what about the nutrients? Can something so processed be good for you?

Unfortunately, making your own fish sticks isn't really a viable daily option (veggie burgers, on the other hand, are simple). We all live in a busy world, and these things in our freezers and cabinets save us time. This is the constant struggle: What is best for you and for the earth versus what is feasible in your life. Buying the least amount of packaged food possible, especially processed packaged food like those energy bars and cookies, is a good idea. These often contain things you don't want in your body, like thickeners, versions of genetically modified soy and corn, stabilizers, and preservatives. The more you eliminate the processed stuff from your diet, the healthier you set yourself up to be. Also: The less you rely on it as a crutch, the better you feel; the more you cook good whole foods, the more money you save, and the more money you can spend on organics. Work to minimize processed packaged foods in your home. Packaged staples that contain one or two ingredients, on the other hand, are mostly fine. Here's how to source the staples carefully.

IMPORTS, IMPORTS EVERYWHERE

It's really a locavore's dilemma that many of my meals involve pasta, cheese, and wine from Italy and France. I've been touting local organic as the most conscious food for pages now, but sometimes it feels like the exotics and the nonlocal are winning the battle. Bananas. Citrus from Texas or Florida when you live in Maine. Flash frozen Alaskan fish for East Coasters. Peek into the kitchen cabinets and suddenly it's global carbon footprint mayhem: peppercorns from India, vanilla beans from Papua New Guinea, Hawaiian sea salt, organic Chilean olive oil, and so on. This is why some locavores choose to give up exotics and imports entirely, or at least stick to a few imported chosen staples, preferably things like spices, which are not overly heavy to transport. If you'd like to reduce the amount of exotic foods you're eating, try making a list of what you can't find locally. Give up what you're willing to give up, consider substitutions (such as local honey or maple syrup for sugar), and factor in how often you're really eating the outliers. You might go through only one vanilla bean a year.

In *Animal, Vegetable, Miracle*, Barbara Kingsolver's lovely memoir of a year spent living off the land, she and her family chose not to give up chocolate, coffee, olive oil, or spices. They were, however, absolutely anti-banana. All long-distance purchases should be chosen as responsibly as local ones. Alice Waters suggests buying only "what has been done more virtuously than others." Items that fall under that umbrella include some fair-trade coffees and chocolates, as well as the types of items made by artisan producers who are Slow Food Presidia members (SlowFoodUSA.org). "These are the people whose products can be shipped and are very special," says Waters, who refers to this as "virtuous globalization."

> **tip**
>
> **Carbon offset.** Adopt as many of the top ten ways to maintain a conscious kitchen as you can (see page 13). They'll more than balance out a little Jamaican allspice.

IN THE CABINET

My own cabinets contain a mix of packaged staples—local when available, but mainly certified organic, and mostly domestic. Most of my grains and the like (bulgur, spelt, oats, quinoa, grits, rice, popcorn, sesame seeds, amaranth, sunflower seeds, nuts, nut butters) are American, but it takes work to figure out what state they hail from. I have local flours and nonlocal flours. Same goes for jams and jellies. Sadly, I'm not entirely sure precisely where most of my dried beans are from, but the cranberry ones are from my CSA. My sea salt, however, is French. And my coconut oil, soba noodles, and soy sauce give me pause—they come from so far away. I buy

CANNED FOOD

Whenever possible, buy what typically comes canned in alternative packaging. Most cans are lined with BPA, a hormone-disrupting chemical (see page 155), that research points to being a smart thing to avoid. BPA had either been banned or was on its way to being banned in certain consumer goods as of press time. Buy beans dried or in glass jars if you can find them. Soup stocks are available in boxes at stores, or make your own (see page 211) and store them in glass jars in your freezer. Two brands claiming to use BPA-free linings in their cans are Vital Choice (VitalChoice.com) and Eden (EdenFoods.com). Because of the acid in tomatoes, even Eden's tomato cans have an epoxy-based lining that may contain small amounts of BPA; otherwise, they would corrode. Whenever I find whole tomatoes in glass, I buy in bulk. BPA levels have even been detected in glass jars (of baby food), probably because it can migrate from the coating on metal lids. All the more reason to minimize exposure where possible and to make your own food from scratch.

---

these infrequently if I'm food-mile-splurging, and always choose Japanese over Chinese-made soba. I gave up on even certified organic food from China out of anger, frustration, and distrust during the Chinese melamine-in-baby-formula scandal of 2008. It was the last straw. I had been reading too many stories of just how tainted their food supply is (not to mention their toy factories). Enough. An even better choice? Some of Eden's soba is, the company says, from North American family farms.

The takeaway here is that there are greener (and often healthier) choices to be made every time you take a package off a store shelf, even if you trust the people who stocked those shelves, and even if the ingredient list is one item only. When shopping, read packages for country- or state-of-origin labels. And look at ingredient lists, even if you think you know what you're buying; additives and sugar pop up in the strangest places.

PASTA

Pasta's a packaged food. Someone (not you) turns the wheat into pasta, packages it, and ships it to a store near you, often from as far away as Italy—though the wheat itself might have come from Canada before being transported to Italy for processing. Sad but true. There are currently no ingredient-origin or country-of-processing labeling requirements to help consumers choose noodle brands that involve less shipping than others. Locally made fresh pasta abounds, but to me it's not the answer since there's still no way to know where the flour or eggs came from. The best a pasta lover can do is find a dried organic brand that explains, either on its label or on a website, where its wheat, preferably whole, is from and where it's processed so you know what sort of trip the product made before getting to you. If your local store carries a bulk organic pasta that tastes good, choose it to cut down on packaging.

tip **Make your own local pasta** from local wheat and your favorite eggs. The Internet is overflowing with instructions. You don't need any special tools (though a hand crank rolling machine is helpful), and it's a great rainy day activity that is also fun for kids.

BREAD

If you have a great bakery near you that turns out bread daily made of the fewest ingredients possible—flour, water, yeast, and maybe salt—and it tastes good, enjoy. I have access to several organic loaves and feel lucky, though I find it difficult to locate bakeries baking bread with local flour, even though local flour is available.

BARBARA KINGSOLVER'S
FRIDAY NIGHT PIZZA

This recipe from *Animal, Vegetable, Miracle* is a great idea for starting a fun family tradition. Making your own dough puts you in charge of the ingredients, gets the kids involved in choosing toppings (hormone- and antibiotic-free cheese, please!), and cuts down on delivery transportation and boxes, not to mention cash.

Makes two 12-inch pizzas

3 teaspoons yeast

½ cups WARM water

3 tablespoons olive oil

1 teaspoon salt

2½ cups white flour

2 cups whole wheat flour

To make crust, dissolve the yeast into the warm water and add oil and salt to that mixture. Mix the flours and knead them into the liquid mixture. Let dough rise for 30 to 40 minutes.

1 cup sliced onions

2 peppers, cut up

While the dough is rising, prepare the sliced onions: a slow sauté to caramelize their sugars makes fresh onions into an amazing vegetable. First sizzle them on medium heat in a little olive oil, until transparent but not browned. Then turn down the burner, add a bit of water if necessary to keep them from browning, and let them cook 10 to 15 minutes more, until they are glossy and sweet. Peppers can benefit from a similar treatment. Once the dough has risen, divide it in half and roll out two round 12-inch pizza crusts on a clean, floured countertop, using your fingers to roll the perimeter into on outer crust as thick as you like. Using spatulas, slide the crusts onto well floured pans or baking stones and spread toppings.

    16 oz. mozzarella, thinly sliced
    2 cups fresh tomatoes in season (or sauce in winter)

OTHER TOPPINGS
    1 tablespoon oregano
    1 teaspoon rosemary
    Olive oil

Layer the cheese evenly over the crust, then scatter the toppings of the week on your pizza, finishing with the spices. If you use tomato sauce (rather than fresh tomatoes), spread that over crust first, then the cheese, then other toppings. Bake pizzas at 425°F for about 15 to 20 minutes, until crust is brown and crisp.

Some of Kingsolver's favorite combinations for summer are:
Mozzarella, fresh tomato slices, and fresh basil, drizzled with olive oil
Mozzarella, chopped tomatoes, caramelized onions, mushrooms
Chopped tomatoes, crumbled feta, finely chopped spinach or chard,
    black olives

Good winter combinations include:
Farmer cheese, chicken, olives, and mushrooms
Tomato sauce, mozzarella, dried peppers, mushrooms, and anchovies

Beware supermarket fresh-baked loaves—these may be partially baked somewhere very far away, frozen, shipped, and then finished off in your store's oven. Ask questions wherever you're purchasing. When buying sliced bread, read ingredient labels carefully. It never contains just the basics and is often loaded with trans fats, chemically processed and enriched flour, preservatives and other chemicals, plus sugars of varying amounts and types (corn syrup versus honey versus molasses). Bread shouldn't last very long, though it can, depending on the type of loaf. If it does, there's likely something in there artificially extending its shelf life. Whole wheat and other whole grain breads are better for you than white, and taste fabulous. If you truly want to know exactly what is in your bread, bake your own. It takes time, but it can be an addictive activity. For recipe inspiration, hit your cookbooks or do a little Googling. Bread machines aren't required. Use your hands (or your kids') to knead.

tip

Don't forget about what goes on your bread—carefully source the butter, cinnamon, nut butters, jams, honey, and what have you. Got stale bread? Make bread crumbs or bread soup—there's a thoughtful version in *Chez Panisse Cooking* by Paul Bertolli with Alice Waters.

SUGAR AND OTHER SWEETENERS

Sweet should be natural. Artificial sweeteners don't belong in a conscious kitchen, which means we can happily avoid any discussions of safety and USDA approval here. When it comes to sugar, fair-trade and organic is a must. "Sugar has to be good, clean, and fair," says Alice Waters. She urges people to watch the documentary *The Price of Sugar* for an in-depth look at why (ThePriceOfSugar.com— the trailer is on YouTube). "It just took my breath away," Waters

THE LIST: SUGAR
A sliding scale of choices from best to worst

• Fair trade, organic, and/or sustainably grown and as unprocessed as possible. Sucanat and brown less-refined sugars contain more nutrients than the soft sugar called "brown." White sugar contains the least. To avoid sugar that was filtered through bones, look for labels stating the product is suitable for vegetarians.

AVOID: Conventional table sugar—white or brown

explains. "I guess I imagined herbicides and pesticides and all of that and unfortunate farming conditions, but I never imagined slavery." Adding a teaspoon to your morning coffee is a political act.

At home, I use a variety of organic brown-colored sugars from our health food market, knowing full well that brown sugar sold in the United States is refined to white and has molasses added back in to turn it varying shades of brown. It's a farce. Truly raw or unrefined sugar is illegal here, just as raw milk is in some states, to protect citizens from impurities and bacteria. The process of refining is done in various ways, and is mainly mechanical, not chemical, though some sugars are filtered through animal by-products (usually bones) and so aren't vegetarian-friendly or friendly for people trying to avoid conventionally raised animals. Refining strips sugar of any useful nutrients it originally had. Brown carries a healthy halo on it, but let's not delude

tip

Sugar can also come from beets. Sounds highly organic, but organic beet sugar is a pretty rare product. Organophiles who indulge yearly in Halloween candy might be getting an unexpected dose of genetically modified beet sugar in their chocolate bars. Reason one zillion and eight to choose organic.

ourselves: Any sugar sold in the United States, even if it is called "raw," has been heated and is at least somewhat refined. I don't turn to sugar for nutrients in the first place, so I'm okay with that, but I don't like misleading labeling.

That said, there are a couple of brownish granulated sugars that can be found in stores that aren't the same thing as moist brown sugar and that are less refined than white granulated sugar. These include demerara, turbinado, muscovado, or what is sold as "raw." These are evaporated cane juice crystals of varying sizes and molasses content that have been spun in a machine. The spinning separates out some of the molasses. Unlike with brown sugar, the molasses has never been totally refined away, then added back in.

In one rather strict vegetarian health food store near where I live, the only sugar cane product they sell is Sucanat. To make this, cane juice is dehydrated and turned into granules, instead of being crystallized. It has a considerably higher molasses content than the crystallized sugars, and is therefore marketed as a source of good-for-you things like iron and potassium.

High fructose corn syrup (HFCS) isn't technically artificial, but it's so processed it's also not technically natural. I treat it like it's artificial and avoid it—an act that takes skill, as it's in just about everything from packaged processed foods to ketchup to

---

ORGANIC CORN SYRUP

There is such a thing as certified organic corn syrup. It's made from non-GM corn that wasn't sprayed with chemical fertilizers and pesticides, and is processed into syrup without chemicals, additives, or artificial flavors. It's not something anyone should be guzzling daily, but it does provide flexibility to organic-interested home bakers, not to mention manufacturers of processed packaged organic food.

THE BUZZ ABOUT BEES

Honey bees are a hot topic in the environmental community. For several years bees have been vanishing from their hives with seemingly no explanation. Researchers have dubbed this "colony collapse disorder" and link it to a combination of factors, including a virus, parasitic mites, and pesticide exposure. More research is needed. The disorder has resulted in honey shortages and higher prices, but there's an even bigger issue at play. We all need bees to pollinate our food supply (conventional and organic), so it's crucial to support the beekeepers working hard on keeping local populations healthy by buying honey even if it costs a few extra dollars. I get mine from my CSA farmer during growing season and from local markets in winter.

yogurt to juice. But if you're eating whole foods and not drinking soda, you're less likely to encounter it. My reasons for avoiding it are myriad: Corn is one of the most genetically modified crops; sugar in general isn't great for you. HFCS has more than a few ties to the obesity epidemic, and should be consumed only in moderation; and mercury, a highly toxic production by-product, has been found in many samples of high fructose corn syrup and brand-name products that contain it. There's a great documentary called *King Corn* that delves into all things corn, including corn syrup, and is well worth a watch (KingCorn.net).

Here are some better nonsugar sweetener choices (look for organic/local/sustainable, of course):

- Honey (see sidebar, above)—buy it at farmers' markets so it's local.
- Maple syrup—buy it at a farmers' market, where it's likely to be the most unprocessed and local.
- Agave nectar—it's like thick simple syrup; perfect for iced tea.
- Molasses—stir into yogurt and baked goods for a not-too-sweet flavor; it can even be used as a supplement for people with low iron.

ALUMINUM-FREE BAKING POWDER

There has long been a health concern with regard to aluminum—in cookware (see page 149) and in things like antiperspirant. Aluminum is sometimes found in baking powder as a leavening agent. The correlation between aluminum ingestion and adverse health effects has never been effectively drawn, and the amount in baking powder is obviously minuscule, but it doesn't seem like a great idea to eat it anyway, especially as there are alternative options. Opt for aluminum-free baking powder, which is pretty widely available. Bonus: Bakers claim it tastes better, less tinny. Makes sense.

BAKING GOODS

We've already covered milk, butter, eggs, and now sugar. But what about other baking necessities? Go for local, organic wheat flours if they're available. In New York, Wild Hive Farm (WildHive Farm.com) stone grinds locally grown organic grains in small batches—everything from hard red spring wheat to spelt to oats to polenta to flours. Poke around farmers' markets and ask at health food stores to see what local spots around you are doing similar work. Many supermarkets now stock organic flour—maybe even whole wheat pastry flour, which can be subbed in for white almost anytime. Meanwhile, all baking-related goods from cream of tartar to cloves are available in organic versions. Keep an eye out for the country-of-origin labels and try to purchase items grown as close to home as possible. Choose glass containers over plastic ones, and buy in bulk when available.

SALT AND PEPPER

The pepper in your mill likely isn't local. Most comes from India, Thailand, Vietnam, Brazil, China, and Sri Lanka. Certain peppercorns are sometimes even treated—green sometimes with sulfur dioxide, red and pink (which aren't technically peppercorns) in some sort of brine. Black, on the other hand, are usually just dried, sometimes in the sun and sometimes mechanically. You'll obviously want to know what the peppercorns at your store were treated with, so you can avoid the questionably processed ones. Buying organic versions, as always, is a good way to ensure best practices.

Used daily, those black flecks add up. Pepper's better half, salt,

---

REFINED VS. UNREFINED: THE IODINE QUESTION

Iodine is crucial for the proper functioning of the thyroid gland. Advocates of refined salt say that consuming table salt—not sea salt—is the only way to get enough iodine in your diet. Maybe. It's certainly the easiest way. There are small amounts of iodine in food like kelp, and in produce grown in iodine-rich regions, such as coastal zones. According to the Mayo Clinic, "Iodine is found in various foods, including seafood, small amounts of iodized salt, and vegetables grown in iodine-rich soils. Iodine-containing mist from the ocean is another important source of iodine." Another reason we need our veggies to have state or even regional origin labels! If you live far from a coastal area, and you choose to supplement your diet with iodized salt, do the research before you go shopping; most refined table salt not only contains iodine but also residues from its purification process as well as anti-caking agents. Some of these chemicals are questionable. Kosher salt tends to lack the additives, but unfortunately it doesn't contain iodine. One compromise is a well-sourced iodized sea salt.

---

is another thing to purchase mindfully. Sea salt is preferable to refined table salt (see page 133). Of course the good stuff, as with pepper, tends to come from faraway places—Hawaii, the Himalayas, and Denmark, for example.

The Skinny on Salt

There is no such thing as organic salt. Salt is a mineral, not a plant, and cannot be certified organic. If you see something called organic salt, buyer beware. Other claims I've seen on salt packages that aren't third-party certified include: ethically sourced; made by renewable wind and solar energy; hand-harvested with wooden rakes only (so no metal touches the salt); from a sheltered area (in other words, it contains less impurities than salt from polluted oceans).

There are, however, two certifications you might find on salt that do truly indicate ecological production and back up the claim that the salt came from a nature reserve (less risk of pollution), was produced by hand, and was not purified. These are Nature & Progrés—NatureEtProgres.org—and Bio-Gro from New Zealand—Bio-Gro.co.nz.

To find certified and pure salt: SaltWorks.us; GreySalt.com; CelticSeaSalt.com; RealSalt.com.

HERBS AND SPICES

Many of the things that give your organic veggies, pastured meat, and carefully chosen fish the perfect flavor—from star anise to varying kinds of peppers—come from exotic locales. Some do not. Study up on what you're buying from afar; you might be surprised to know that you can find versions that are from closer to home. When it comes to herbs, there's plenty of organic, local, fresh variety. My CSA farm even grows hot scotch bonnet peppers, which are typically found in the Caribbean. For the least expensive organic fresh herbs around, set up a small window box of them in the kitchen, or plant a larger herb garden if you have the outdoor space. Use organic soil, top it off with some worm bin compost if available (see page 211), and pick as needed. For all dried staples like bay leaves, cinnamon, fennel and coriander seeds, curry powder, or spice blends, also look for local when possible (why not dry your own homegrown rosemary, thyme, sage, and more?), and make sure to choose organic. Many conventional dried spices are irradiated (see page 18), a process that isn't permitted by organic standards.

VANILLA

Vanilla beans are yet another carbon-footprint-unfriendly exotic; they mainly come from Papua New Guinea and Madagascar. Though they're not exactly as heavy to import as, say, a banana, and they're used infrequently. You might have vanilla in some capacity in your kitchen, be it in bean form, as a flavor in a container of ice cream, or as an extract kept near your baking goods. Beans can be expensive, as they're resource intensive to grow, but at least you know they're real. It turns out that most vanilla flavoring isn't vanilla at all, but rather a synthetic made from a petrochemical or derived from a by-product of the paper industry. To avoid all but the real stuff, look out for any label that says "artificial flavor," "natural

tip

Make your own vanilla extract: Slit open a few beans and place them and 1 cup (organic!) vodka in a small jar in a cool, dark place. Wait a month or even two, shaking the jar every once in a while. Voilà.

flavor," "vanilla flavor" or "vanillin," especially in things like ice cream or chocolate. Invest instead in real organic pure vanilla extract, or the beans themselves. Stored in a cool, dark place, pods can last for two years (one year is a better idea).

CHOCOLATE

All of this careful shopping and label reading can really wear a person down on occasion. Overwhelming! Good news: It's time to taste chocolate. Go dark enough and you can write it off as a health food. (Sort of.) Plan to spend more than what an average candy bar costs, but with good reason. Like coffee, conventional chocolate production is tough on the rain forests and brutal on workers (some of them children). Which means fair-trade certification is a must when it comes to chocolate, along with organic. Herewith, a list of the brands mentioned in my unscientific eco-chocolate poll, conducted while researching this book. Extra good news: More and more people are jumping on the sustainable chocolate bandwagon, so the pool of conscious chocolates available across the country

ANOTHER CHOCOLATE CERTIFICATION

As with coffee, if when looking for organic and Fair Trade Certified chocolate, you spy a Rainforest Alliance Certified label, snag that bar. The seal means the cocoa is responsibly grown and harvested, and that the farm has met a series of environmental as well as social standards. These include improved water and soil quality and worker access to education and health care. One sustainable bar that sports this certification is Vintage Plantations (VintagePlantations.com). In 2009, Rainforest Alliance even began working with the Mars Corporation to move toward more sustainable practices, with a long-term end goal of becoming certified.

is growing. Check the following websites to purchase or to find retailers near you. All of these are widely available, especially in chains like Whole Foods, health food stores, and specialty markets:

- Vere Chocolates (VereChocolate.com): dark bars and more, handmade in New York City from sustainably grown, pesticide-free Ecuadorian cocoa beans and very little sugar. Rainforest Alliance certified.

- Kallari (Kallari.com): organic dark chocolate bars from a self-governed coalition of Amazon artists and organic cocoa producers. Founded in 1997 with less than fifty families in Ecuador, the association has now grown to include more than eight hundred families. It's the ultimate tale of a cooperative currently making fair wages for organic production instead of earning unfair wages for logging rain forests or selling their land.

- Green & Black's (GreenAndBlacks.com): these certified organic bars get thumbs-up for being widely available and relatively inexpensive. Purists bemoan that it's now owned by Cadbury-Schweppes. Currently only their Maya Gold bar and cocoa powder are Fair Trade Certified.

- Divine Chocolate (DivineChocolate.com): farmer-owned, Fair Trade Certified, and dedicated to improving the livelihood of small-scale cocoa farmers in Ghana.

- Theo Chocolate (TheoChocolate.com): organic, Fair Trade Certified; made in Seattle.

- Equal Exchange (EqualExchange.coop): Fair Trade Certified since 1986, comprised of more than forty small farmer co-ops in twenty-two countries that produce chocolate plus tea and coffee. The cocoa beans are Peruvian and Dominican.

- Endangered Species Chocolate (www.ChocolateBar.com): these come in "natural" and organic versions—natural may not be grown according to organic principles but it is, they contend, ethically traded, shade-grown, and single-origin. Their website has info on how the company is attempting to green its operation, and the bar wrappers are recycled paper with water-based ink. They donate a portion of net profits to "support species, habitat, and humanity."

OIL

A drizzle of high-quality olive oil is indispensable in many dishes. Seeking out pure olive oil, independent of ecological issues, takes a little extra vigilance, as some producers are looking to cash in on its cache by selling fraudulent oil—they mix together soybean and low-grade olive oils, then sell it with a label claiming it's extra virgin. In 2007, FDA investigators and U.S. Marshals seized more than ten thousand cases of adulterated olive oil from storage facilities in New York and New Jersey. Connecticut and California have since enacted standards to protect consumers from this kind of fraud, and other states will surely follow. If your state doesn't have a law in place, buy from stores and people you trust. Ask questions. And poke around to see if there is an olive oil cooperative near you—it's like a CSA but for olive oil.

JUST SAY NO TO GMO

Corn, canola (rapeseed), and soybean oils are the biggest production oils around and are the main ingredients in commercial salad dressings. They are also the oils most likely to be made from genetically modified crops. USDA organic standards ban the use of genetically modified ingredients. Organic versions of all three do exist, as do glass bottles of prefab organic bottled dressing containing them, though making your own dressing always means fewer additives—and it's tastier, too.

CONDIMENTS

Where I live, my CSA grows soybeans, and there's local tofu, but not local soy sauce. (Please e-mail me if I'm wrong.) If you're a soy sauce, hot sauce, chili oil, ketchup, or any other sort of bottled-flavor junkie, see if you can find your elixir in a glass-bottled small batch, locally grown and prepared variety. Don't forget to read the labels—organic or not—before heading to the checkout; condiments are prime homes for snuck-in sugars and added preservatives you might want to avoid.

The organic seal on cooking or finishing oils—olive plus corn, soy, peanut, and more—doesn't inherently protect consumers from fraudulent blending, but it does protect against pesticide residue and environmental harm. Dedicated locavores bypass oils that aren't grown near them for those that are. Coconut or sesame oils might be too far-flung, but maybe grapeseed, safflower, sunflower, or pumpkin seed oils are closer compromises. No matter what you choose, always read labels for additives or unexpected ingredients.

VINEGAR

The options here are bountiful. Maybe you're a sherry person or a balsamic lover, or you've found a handcrafted vinegar at the farmers' market that adds the right kick to your CSA greens. You might even want to try making your own—this is very doable with leftover red wine (see box on page 140). I like a wide variety of vinegars but haven't had much luck in locating local versions—even though I live near many apple orchards, the cider vinegar at my health food store carries no mention on the label of where the cider apples came from. It says manufactured in close-to-me Brooklyn and certified in California. Where something is certified rarely indicates where it was grown. Would that someone would bother to map the apples.

Unfortunately, some conventional vinegars on the shelves might actually be made from distilled corn, wood, or even petroleum. Lovely. If you're someone who doesn't want to be eating GM corn or petroleum products, look for organic. Price isn't always an accurate gauge of purity; that aforementioned certified organic raw cider vinegar only set me back three dollars, but its organic seal proves it's not the scary stuff. When in doubt, read labels, as always.

Leaded Vinegar?

In California, some vinegars carry warning labels about their lead content, even though—of course—the industry says the levels are low enough to be safe. The labels are thanks to California's Proposition 65 legislation (aka the Safe Drinking Water and Toxic

DIY VINEGAR

Using wine dregs to make red wine vinegar is not terribly difficult but does require patience and time. It can be confusing to get going, as everyone seems to have a different "recipe" for how—and in what— to make it happen. If you're interested, do a little Internet research, including learning about something called "mother of vinegar," and make sure to go here: GangOfPour.com/diversions/vinegar. Devotees swear homemade red wine vinegar is both crisper and more subtle than the commercial stuff. What could be greener than creating something spectacular and useful out of almost nothing?

Enforcement Act of 1986—www.CalProp65.com), which helps consumers know exactly what's in their food (and beyond) and can sometimes, critics say, be overzealous. Still, who wouldn't prefer to be in the know? Activists say no level of lead is safe. Some say the lead in the vinegar comes from the soil (many California grapes are grown close to highways and there's residual lead in soil from back when gasoline was leaded); others point to the manufacturing process, and still others say this stems from lead in the old plumbing in Italy and pertains only to Italian balsamic. None of these explanations is comforting, nor do they help put this into a larger context. Anything grown in soil that contains lead could also have the heavy metal in it. But not everything—including wine and grape juice—is labeled this way. Why not? And why is the specific lead level in vinegar enough to merit the Proposition 65 warning? Vinegar is manufactured similarly to wine, so if it's a question of manufacturing, this might not be great news for oenophiles either. Consumers need more—and clearer—information. There are companies like O Olive Oil now starting to market balsamic with lower levels of lead than even Prop 65 requires, one option if you're not comfortable living with yet another unanswerable food conundrum.

CHAPTER EIGHT

pots, pans, food storage, and tabletop

NOW THAT YOUR LARDER, CABINET, GARDENS, AND MAYBE even root cellar are stocked with the best, greenest, most delicious whole foods and other ingredients you saw fit to source, it's time to turn your attention to your kitchen proper, specifically what you're cooking in and on, and what you're storing and serving food in.

When it comes to a conscious kitchen, less is always more. Transitioning your kitchen from not-so-green to greener might actually be about taking some platters and utensils out of rotation and clearing out what you're currently using rather than buying much new. Most kitchens are stuffed with an unnecessary assortment of random equipment, from milk frothers to egg slicers to smoothie makers. If you're downsizing, an eco-friendly way to get rid of your (nontoxic) castoffs is to offer them to friends and family members who might be interested in them, donate them to a local thrift store, or give them away via Freecycle.org. One caveat: Don't do this with nonstick items; these should just be thrown away (see page 146). If you do buy something new, always go for the best possible quality, even if it costs more up front. A durable item that lasts twenty years or longer—be it a big-ticket item like a pot or set of knives or a small gadget like a spatula—is greener than cheap tempting-in-the-store items that break after two experiments and wind up as landfill waste.

WHAT YOU'RE COOKING IN AND ON

All cooking materials have pros and cons—how well they work, how long they last, how the environment was affected when their materials were extracted from the earth and when they were manufactured, and how they impact human health. Some are arguably better across the board. When looking to add iron to a diet, doctors and nutritionists will suggest cooking in cast-iron pans; small amounts of it leach from the pan into food as it cooks. Iron is safe, but there are a whole host of questionable materials lining other pots and pans—especially nonstick—that you do not want seeping into your food. Thankfully these are easy to avoid. The best tried-and-true cookware materials are:

- Cast iron
- Stainless steel
- Enamel-coated cast iron (like Le Creuset)

The latter two can be quite expensive, but cast iron itself is not. Lodge, the widely available American cast-iron kitchenware manufacturer, also makes a not-too-pricey line of the enamel-coated version (LodgeMFG.com).

Cast Iron

Cast iron has been used for cooking for thousands of years. Before you spend twenty dollars or less on a new cast-iron pan, look in your shelves, or your relatives' cabinets, or poke around thrift stores to see if you happen on a well-worn find—they seem to lurk everywhere. An aged pan is great because the surface of cast iron

CAST-IRON CARE

TO "SEASON" A CAST-IRON ITEM:

If buying new, check the manufacturer's instructions. For all other cast iron, apply a thin, even coating of fat inside and out with a cloth. Vegetable oil, trans-fat-free shortening, lard, and/or bacon grease are considered best; avoid butter because it burns. Place the piece in a 350°F oven. Bake it for one hour (you can wipe excess fat off the pan after fifteen minutes, or bake it upside down and let the drippings fall onto a baking sheet placed below it). Then turn off the oven, and leave the pan in there until it's cool. To reseason an old or improperly cured item, clean it well with hot water and a scouring pad, dry it, then season. And as long as you've got the oven going for that long, make some food in a separate dish at the same time.

TO CLEAN CAST IRON:

Either wipe the pan out, or use hot water and a stiff brush shortly after cooking. Don't use soap or scouring pads, which break down the seasoning. If the pan is really greasy, a wee drop of soap won't kill it—you can always reseason. For truly stuck-on food, try boiling a little water in the pan to loosen it, then use a stiff brush. Dry well. Don't soak it in water or store food in it. For more helpful care tips, see Lodge's website, LodgeMFG.com.

becomes more nonstick over time. Rust spots can be cleaned and reseasoned. I have several sizes, and use them for everything from eggs to skillet breads. Bonus: Once heated, they retain heat so well that you can turn down your stove and use less energy to finish cooking. They also transition beautifully from stovetop to oven and even to broiler. Two caveats: You must use fat (oil, butter) so your food won't stick to cast iron; also, while you can cook tomatoes and other acidic food in cast iron, a pan that isn't well seasoned may react with the acid in the food and impart a subtle metallic taste to the dish.

Stainless Steel

Cast iron is heavy. This makes it a tough choice for cooking something you want to be able to pick up and swirl, like a sauce. For this kind of freedom in a safe cooking material, opt for stainless steel. Look through your pots and pans; you might already have some. If shopping for new, avoid stainless-steel pots and pans constructed with cores or exteriors made with other metals, like aluminum. If you can't locate such an item, make sure the interior of the pan—the part where your food will touch—is only stainless steel. One step up the luxury chain that is safe is copper-core or copper-bottom stainless steel, which conducts heat better than pure stainless and can save cooking energy, but can be quite expensive.

tip

Do not store foods that are highly acidic, like cooked tomatoes or rhubarb, in stainless steel, as the acid can cause the metal to break down into your food over time. Cooking acidic food in stainless steel is perfectly safe.

Enamel-Coated Cast Iron

Put one (or two) of these pricey pots on your birthday or holiday wish list now, or ask family members for hand-me-downs. Enamel is a fused hard coating of fine glass particles. Enamel-coated cast iron has all of the energy benefits of cast iron, plus a more slippery (but not completely nonstick) and totally nonreactive cooking surface. The dutch ovens are perfect for soups, stews, and sauces, and are ideal for one-pot meals. I use mine so frequently that it lives on the stovetop; there's no point in putting it away. Treat these pots and pans well and according to the manufacturer's instructions so the enamel won't wear down, scratch, or chip, and they'll last forever.

Nonstick

Nonstick is, forgive me, a sticky topic. Until recently, most non-stick cookware was made with perfluorooctanoic acid (PFOA), a perfluorochemical that has been linked to cancer (an EPA advisory council has designated it a "likely carcinogen"), infertility, and complications during pregnancy. PFOA contaminates and persists in the environment, has been shown to cause adverse effects in animal testing, and has been found at low levels in the blood of 98 percent of the general U.S. population. The chemical remains in the human body for years, and levels build up over time.

In the kitchen, scratched pans are the main source of exposure. If you've ever had a nonstick pan, you know they scratch and flake pretty easily. Perfluorochemicals also break down at high temperatures—temperatures that people can and do reach in their own homes, especially if they preheat their pans, or put them under the broiler (which you're not supposed to do with nonstick). The fumes can cause acute flulike symptoms if inhaled by humans (this is known as polymer fume fever) and can be extremely toxic to birds. There have been reports of bird deaths linked to nonstick pan fumes. Talk about the canary in the coal mine. In studies, rats have also died after inhaling the chemical.

In 2005, DuPont settled with the EPA for $16.5 million for allegedly withholding PFOA health risk information. This included a $10.25 million penalty and a pledge to spend $6.25 million more on environmental projects. The EPA also called on DuPont and six other chemical companies to voluntarily eliminate PFOA and similar substances from plant emissions and products by 2015.

PFOA is an ingredient in the manufacture of PTFE (polytetrafluoroethylene), a polymer used in cookware and other nonstick applications. Brand names that contain it (and other chemicals) include Teflon and Silverstone. But once this chemical is out of use, consumers will be stuck with unknown chemical replacements

PACKAGING'S DIRTY LITTLE NONSTICK SECRET

You may find yourself eating less and less takeout and packaged snacks as you get more involved with sourcing your own ingredients, and even making your own pizza (page 126). If you're still eating takeout—a little or a lot—check out the packaging the next time it arrives at your door. Some paper and cardboard containers are kept from leaking en route by a PFOA-based coating. They repel grease, and feel slick to the touch. If you've popped microwave popcorn, you'll know the feeling from the inside of those bags. It's not exactly what you want touching—and getting into—your hot food. Order in from places that aren't using PFOA-coated boxes, and air or stove-top pop your popcorn. Some butter wrappers are similarly coated. Call manufacturers to ask what, precisely, your food container is lined in, and, if it's the bad stuff, let them know that you'd prefer it lined in something better. If you can choose different takeout containers (order from somewhere else), or food wrapping materials, do.

---

that might not be safe, either. Less toxic is still toxic. Nonstick pots and pans are not labeled with which chemicals they contain. You have to dig deep and go to manufacturers' websites to figure these out, and the information is inevitably harder to find than it should be. Better to avoid by choosing other, safer materials.

By not buying pans made with nonstick coatings, you're also voting with your dollars against the companies that make these chemicals. So what to do with the nonstick you're currently using? Throw it away ASAP. In the trash. You can't even recycle it, though I have seen some creative at-home recycling I'm not sure I condone—one friend uses her nonstick pasta pot as a potty for her children. If you're going to hold on to it, at least throw out any scratched pans. Treat unscratched ones carefully by using utensils that will never scratch them, by never putting them on high heat, and by washing and drying them like they're newborns. I think getting rid of them is a safer, more practical, less worrisome option. The unknown is too vast, the manufacture is too environmentally destructive, and safer alternatives abound.

The New Nonstick

Despite the well-documented health issues, people cling to nonstick because of its ease, and because you can cook in it using very little fat, with very little cleanup. Thankfully the marketplace has responded to continued demand for greener, safer versions of nonstick surfaces. As always, read the fine print and do the research to make sure whatever newfangled cooking surface you're considering doesn't actually contain other chemicals that should be avoided. This is an arena where greenwashing—the whitewashing that occurs all too often in the green products area—can rear its ugly head. Greenpan, for example, is one PFOA- and PTFE-free newcomer lined with something called Thermolon, but it does use controversial nanotechnology as well as silicone (see page 151), both of which raise potential health concerns. Cuisinart's Green Gourmet line is ceramic-based (instead of petroleum-based), and free of PTFE and PFOA; its stainless handles are said to be made from 70 percent recycled stainless steel. There are also now enamel-coated frying pans. Surely other "green" cooking options will continue to flood the market. Just remember that the most conscious pots and pans are the toxin-free durable items you already own. New technology doesn't always stand the test of time. Use what you know to be safe.

Aluminum

There has been concern and confusion over the years about aluminum's link to Alzheimer's disease, enough to warrant studies, attention, and lingering concern. No direct link has been established, and everything I've read about cooking in aluminum pots and pans makes them sound safe, ditto for anodized aluminum. Cookware made from it is relatively cheap and conducts heat well, so people like it. The process of anodizing is very chemical-heavy (basically, aluminum is put in a chemical bath and an electrical current is applied, which makes it hard and corrosion-resistant). Many aluminum pans have nonstick surfaces, so if you have a set, figure out what's coating it. Cooking and/or storing acidic foods (tomato sauce and the like) in aluminum pots and pans makes it more likely there will be aluminum in your food, especially if there are scrapes in the pan's cooking surface. It also can discolor food and affect its taste. Do not use the cookware at all if it has gouges. The mining of bauxite and the refining and manufacture of the resulting aluminum are more energy-intensive than the processing and manufacture of copper and stainless steel. I favor other materials than aluminum in my kitchen.

Copper

While this metal conducts heat extremely well, copper cookware tends to be prohibitively expensive. Because too much copper isn't good for us, copper pans tend to be coated with another metal that prevents it from coming into direct contact with food. Make sure this lining is stainless steel or another safe material. Don't use copper if it isn't lined or if the lining is scratched.

BAKEWARE

The best baking materials are similar to those for pots and pans:

- Cast iron
- Stainless steel
- Glass
- Ceramic (lead-free)
- Real cook-safe clay

tip

Do not put glass on the stovetop, and be careful where you set it down when you take it out of the oven. If it hits a spot of cold water on your counter when red-hot, it can shatter.

Cast iron is well suited to baking muffins and breads. Ovenproof glass (like Pyrex) as well as ceramic work well for pies. Stainless-steel baking sheets and ovenproof glass dishes can be used for just about anything. None of these are nonstick, so they all require a little greasing depending on what you're baking. Bonus: Glass and ceramic can do the same oven

POTTERY AND LEAD

Have you seen that cool-looking black clay pottery that claims to go from stovetop to oven to microwave? It's said to be lead-free. But not all vessels are, especially if they were picked up on a far-flung vacation, or if they are very old pieces found at an antique store. When in doubt—whether you're baking, serving, or drinking out of a ceramic item—test it with LeadCheck, a widely available and reliable DIY kit that is EPA recognized. If you have a plate that's a bit worn in one place, do the test there. If there are no worn parts, and have reason to be extra suspicious about the item you're testing, scratch the glaze on the underbelly, and swab there. The product is available through Home Depot, Lowe's, Ace Hardware, and other retailers. For more information: LeadCheck.com.

work at lower temperatures (by about 25 degrees) than their metal counterparts.

Always avoid nonstick baking sheets, for all of the reasons just mentioned when discussing nonstick pans. If you have some already in use, toss them.

Aluminum and Silicone

Many bakers prefer aluminum sheets and say it conducts heat better and more evenly than stainless steel. Unfortunately, it does best lined with parchment paper, which creates a lot of waste other baking materials don't. As it may corrode into salty or acidic foods, aluminum sheets don't do solid double duty in a conscious kitchen, whereas those glass and ceramic pans can roast veggies or bake a frittata when not turning out cookies, and the stainless-steel sheets can go in the broiler with a rosemary-kissed pork chop.

Silicone is arguably the most popular baking material of the

ECO-LINERS

It's a good idea, environmentally speaking, to avoid using paper products in the kitchen. When baking, you can simply grease your pan. If you insist on using paper liners for cupcakes, or parchment paper under your cookies, buy unbleached versions. Bleach is used to make paper fibers white and bright, which is what most consumers deem clean and pretty. Unfortunately, when chlorine is used to bleach paper, carcinogens (called dioxins) can form. Some parchment papers are also coated with quilon, a sort of nonstick lining made by DuPont from chrome, a heavy metal. If you're okay with using silicone, an alternative to quilon-lined is silicone-coated parchment paper. A company called If You Care makes it, as well as unbleached cupcake liners, recycled aluminum foil (it's pricey, which will motivate you to use it less often), and coffee filters (IfYouCare.com). Using clear, reusable silicone baking mats creates less waste.

---

moment, and understandably so—it's nonstick with no extra coating, flexible, neat-looking, and versatile. While the FDA-approved food grade version is made mainly of sand and oxygen (safe and safe), there are additives that make it colorful and flexible. These aren't disclosed on labels, so consumers don't know exactly what they're getting, and the effects on health are unknown. Meanwhile, silicone can also let off fumes if improperly cured by the manufacturer, and can melt at as low as 428°F. Home ovens, as we all know, can be set to 500°F.

Silicone has still other pros and cons: It's long lasting, and it eliminates the need for toss-after-baking items like aluminum foil or parchment paper. But it's not easy to recycle when you're done with it. The one silicone item I ever bought, years before I was questioning plastic, lost its shape very quickly and therefore was in a landfill early on. There are certainly other proven, dependable baking-safe materials that last longer and can be recycled at the end of their useful life.

KNIVES

I've seen knives marketed as eco-friendly—ones with very cool-looking ceramic blades, and others with "eco wood" or sustainable bamboo handles. These pique my interest but I'm not in the market; I already have knives that will last for a very long time. In fact, the greenest thing you can do in this arena is to invest good cash on durable tried-and-true knives, and then take good care of them so they will last a lifetime, rather than winding up as kitchen clutter and eventually garbage. Forged high-carbon steel knives are safe (they've been made this way for centuries) and have the longest-lasting blades that are easy to sharpen at home. Stainless steel isn't as easy to sharpen, but it won't stain or rust. You can get by with a chef's knife, but it's helpful to also have a paring knife, a serrated bread knife, a cleaver (for those big cuts of CSA meat, and hacking up your own whole chickens, which is less expensive than buying parts), and a pair of kitchen shears. A slicing knife is also nice for all of those farmers' market tomatoes and organic roasts.

CUTTING BOARDS

You might have noticed a theme emerging in these pages: I'm not fond of plastic. Which is why I chop on wood, and sometimes bamboo, and have phased plastic cutting boards out of my kitchen. It is a myth that wood is less sanitary than plastic, especially when dealing with raw poultry and meat. If anything, it's the opposite. Hard woods have inherently antibacterial properties, and minor cuts in the surface tend to close up, leaving bacteria with no place to live, which isn't the case with plastic. I've read various accounts of wood boards having less bacteria present than plastic one day post–chicken cutting. To avoid cross-contamination, you can maintain one wood board for raw meat only.

OTHER CONSCIOUS CHOPPING MATERIALS

- Bamboo—read the fine print to learn how and where this renewable wonder plant was grown and harvested.
- Paperboard—Preserve makes an FSC-certified 100 percent post-consumer recycled paper cutting board that they say goes in the dishwasher: PreserveProducts.com.
- Glass and stainless steel—you can chop on these safe materials, but they are, unfortunately, extremely harsh on the knives you want to last a lifetime.

If you're going for wood, choose a hard—never particleboard—sustainable and preferably local wood (Vermont, for example, is a lot closer to me than Indonesia). See if your kitchen supply store stocks wood boards that are certified sustainably harvested by the Forest Stewardship Council (FSC.org), or search for them online. Make sure the wood hasn't been varnished or treated with anything you don't want flaking off into your food; it should be bare. Wood boards cost more up front than plastic, but they are made from a renewable resource and, unlike plastic, will last forever if treated well. When they start to look too dinged up, you can have them resurfaced, which you cannot do with plastic. Wood boards have to be washed by hand, never in a dishwasher, and cannot be left to soak. Rub them with coarse salt to further clean and deodorize them while smoothing out the wood. Most manufacturers suggest oiling them before use, and when they look dry (a few times a year). The most common oil for treating wood boards is mineral, but organic food grade linseed and tung oil are much more eco- (and health) friendly. Do not cure wood boards with vegetable oils; they will go rancid.

WHY TO AVOID PLASTIC IN THE KITCHEN

Allow me to list the reasons. It is made from petroleum, a nonrenewable resource. It takes a tremendous amount of energy to produce. Depending on what kind of plastic it is, it might release carcinogenic toxins into the environment during manufacture or disposal. It isn't readily recyclable, despite all of the recycling bins on American curbs. It might be easy in the moment, but it's not durable long-term. Several plastics approved for use with food and drink contain a whole host of questionable chemicals that can and do make their way into the food we eat and the liquids we drink. These chemicals make plastic hard, colorful, shatterproof, even flexible, and have been linked in many serious scientific studies to endocrine system disruption, kidney failure, and even cancers. The current media darlings of these chemicals (the ones getting the most attention) are bisphenol-A (BPA) and phthalates, though there are others.

BPA

A hormone disrupter (it mimics estrogen) that has the FDA, Health Canada, and the United States Department of Health and Human Services' National Toxicology Program, among other entities, in a tizzy, and parents and hikers across the nation switching their baby and water bottles to BPA-free versions. Manufacturers have taken consumer temperature and are busily marketing "safe" plastic products. Unfortunately, some of the resulting BPA-free items contain other chemicals that are new to this arena and haven't exactly stood the test of time. Because BPA is so pervasive—it can also be found in can linings, dental fillings, and even newspaper ink—we're currently being exposed to higher levels of it than was previously deemed safe. Other studies have linked BPA to heart disease, learning and memory issues, and diabetes. As of press time, Canada as well as some states, cities, and counties in the United States have banned it in certain consumer products, or have begun the process of banning it, with more clearly to come. Many environmental organizations and government representatives are pushing for a more pervasive federal ban.

tip

There's some concern that the coating on metal tops for glass jars contains BPA. Don't fill food, especially acidic food, to the top. Or buy glass jars with rubber seals and glass tops.

PHTHALATES

This family of chemicals, which make plastic flexible (among many other things), are endocrine disrupters and reproductive toxicants.

They are currently being voluntarily removed or banned from everything from nail polish to neonatal tubing to toys. They're less ubiquitous in a kitchen than BPA but are likely found in certain plastics (like meat and cheese wrappings) as well as PVC (vinyl) flooring and even in cleaning-product fragrance.

While many reputable environmental health experts believe there are safe plastics on the market—notably those labeled #2, #4, and #5—many kitchen items, from spatulas to baby bottles to appliances, are not labeled with a number, typically found inside a triangle of recycling arrows on the bottom of the product. Consumers are therefore left either to purchase blindly or to call up manufacturers to figure out what these items are made of. I have made these phone calls on countless occasions. If you go this route, you will likely be connected and reconnected to fifteen different customer service people until someone takes your name and number and doesn't call you back. Apparently many people do not know what they're selling, and certain items are made batch by batch, and the materials sometimes change.

tip

If you are using plastic, do not put it in the microwave (see page 180). Whatever chemicals it contains will get into your food.

Plastics that fall under the numbers 3, 6, and 7 are the bad boys (see list, page 158), but within these classifications there are shades of gray. I always avoid these, especially PVC/vinyl (#3). It's universally referred to in green circles as "poison plastic," because from manufacture to disposal it is extremely environmentally destructive, and because of its known and scary health risks. (Make a note to rent the documentary *Blue Vinyl*—BlueVinyl.org—a palatable, informative, and powerful way to learn about vinyl).

There are plastics that are probably okay, but I'm not interested in being a guinea pig. Health Canada tested for and found BPA in plastic sold as "BPA-free." Who is to say when the next found-in-plastic chemical scandal will erupt? Maybe it will be about plastic #1 (PET), which is what most bottled water comes in. It's long been considered safe, but in 2009 German scientists found that it, too, may leach hormone disruptors into its contents.

Here's the thing—it is much, much easier to avoid plastic than it is to worry about it, or to make a zillion phone calls to try to find out which plastic, say, your kid's spoon is made of, or to memorize which numbers are okay and which aren't. There is no point in wondering what might be lurking in your plastic items when there are excellent, easy-to-find alternatives. Plastic is quite simple to circumvent when it comes to kitchen items. Let me type that again: Plastic is easy to avoid.

AVOIDING PLASTIC: A PRIMER

To avoid plastic, shift your mind-set. The rest will follow. We're all so accustomed to plastic containers that we forget there are many other options. But we're a nation that is currently working on breaking off our codependent relationship with plastic shopping bags, and slowly but surely coming around to understand that bottled water is an environmentally unfriendly rip-off (see page 96). These both involve shifting your mind-set, too. So take it one step further, and fill your conscious kitchen with wood, glass, stainless steel, and (lead-free) ceramic. Of course plastic will remain in some iteration. We all live in the modern world. But it won't be the most common material you or your food will come into contact with. And that's a great step in the right direction.

For food storage, I have three words for you: Glass. Canning. Jars. They're convenient and can be found in supermarkets and hardware stores. "Glass is melted sand, you just can't improve on

THE LIST: PLASTICS
A sliding scale of choices from best to worst

ONE CAVEAT: Just because a plastic is generally considered safe doesn't mean it's easy to recycle, nor does it mean it's safe to reuse with food, or heat up in a dishwasher or a microwave. Always look for safety information labels on packaging, or check with the manufacturer.

• Not using plastic at all
• Current science shows #2, #4, and #5 to be the safest plastics:

  #2 (HDPE or high-density polyethylene), a hard plastic used for everything from milk jugs to cleaning product containers, is presently being used as one of the replacements for bisphenol-A containing polycarbonate (#7) in baby and reusable water bottles.

  #4 (LDPE or low-density polyethylene), a soft plastic widely used for food storage bags, plastic shopping bags, and squeezable bottles.

  #5 (PP or polypropylene), a versatile plastic that is used for bottle tops, yogurt and food storage containers, plus baby bottles.

• #1 PET or PETE (polyethylene terephthalate) is the most commonly used plastic for everything from water bottles to food containers, and is meant for one use only. A few studies regarding PET safety concerns are starting to pop up—use it in moderation.

AVOID:
• #3 (polyvinyl chloride, aka vinyl or PVC), aka "poison plastic." It has been linked to cancer, and contains hormone-disrupting phthalates and possibly lead. In a kitchen it can be found in food containers, some plastic wraps, place mats, and tablecloths.
• #6 (polystyrene) contains hormone disruptors, which can get in your food, and has been linked to cancer. It's most recognizable

as Styrofoam, but also comes in a harder version used for things like children's yogurt cups (these contain very low amounts of styrene). The EPA warns styrene can be harmful to human health, and certain cities have banned it.

- #7 (other, a catch-all), this classification is for any and all plastics that don't fall under #1 to #6, and can include polycarbonate, the hard plastic used mainly for bottles (water and baby) that contains bisphenol-A.

A SECOND CAVEAT: Corn- or sugar-derived plastic also falls under #7, and is considered safe. But its not as ecological as it sounds. It's made primarily from GM plants, which require quite a bit of fertilizer, and the process to turn them into plastic involves much work plus chemicals to stabilize them. It gets a green (marketing) halo because it is considered biodegradable but it only biodegrades under specific conditions. And most recyclers don't recycle it. So mostly it winds up in landfills. Just like petroleum-derived plastic.

that," says *Animal, Vegetable, Miracle* author Barbara Kingsolver. "Mason jars are wonderful for everything." Glass even works in the freezer—just allow room for liquid to expand. Other plastic-alternative glass and ceramic containers are sold at every chain store from IKEA to Crate and Barrel. Some have plastic tops, others don't. Don't fret if yours do, just don't fill them to the point where the food touches the plastic.

For utensils, choose stainless steel or silver. "Cocktail" and/or espresso spoons are the perfect size for kids. In terms of gadgets, remember that everything plastic comes in other versions, too— use them, especially if they're glass, wood, safe ceramic, or stainless steel.

When shopping, seek out items not packaged in plastic and

REUSABLE TOTES

Carrying around reusable shopping bags, stashing them in the trunk of your car or the basket of your bike, or all three has become chic. Hallelujah! I have read that only 20 percent of paper bags in use are recycled, and we all know the situation with plastic bags. There are a zillion places to get (very cute) reusable bags for whatever your needs. Whether you want a sack made out of old PET bottles that folds into a tiny square to throw into your purse, briefcase, or carry-on bag, or a giant sturdy hemp tote, options abound. So much so that I keep joking canvas bag recycling might soon have to be instituted. You should also invest in reusable produce bags. They come in all shapes and sizes so you won't have to rip plastic bags off the supermarket roll for your lettuce or your bulk rice any longer. Mine are organic cotton. Stash in the bigger bags so you won't forget them. Some resources:

- EcoBags.com
- GreenFeet.com
- BagguBag.com
- ReusableBags.com
- ChicoBag.com

you'll have less to throw away or recycle. Whole fruits, vegetables, and bulk items like rice, nuts, and dried fruit can be bagged by you in cloth produce bags (see above). Juice, nut butters, jams, maple syrup, and the like come in glass. Buy eggs in paper/cardboard cartons over Styrofoam or clear plastic. Chemicals in plastic are more likely to migrate into foods with high fat content like cheese or meat. Unfortunately it's difficult to locate either out of plastic. See if you can at least avoid meat sold on foam trays.

To avoid using and tossing plastic when out of your kitchen—either at work or on a picnic—always pack real silverware and something reusable to eat off of (lead-free enamel-coated metal is very light), plus reusable water bottles, and so on.

Overall, don't bother being obsessive. Short of living in a non-plastic bubble, you will clearly encounter some plastic. The point is to—when you can—minimize exposure to questionable chemicals that build up in our bodies over time, as well as to avoid being involved with the environmental impact of their manufacture and disposal.

PLASTIC BAGGIES, WRAP, AND WAX PAPER

A few years back, I wrote an eco-comparison (aka a life-cycle assessment—see below) of plastic bags versus waxed paper bags for the Green Guide. After doing the research, my personal conclusion was to use only unbleached waxed paper bags when not using recyclable containers. But as the printed article was about energy, its conclusion was that plastic bags had a slight

---

LIFE-CYCLE ASSESSMENTS

To my mind, there's nothing more confusing than a life-cycle assessment (LCA). According to the National Risk Management Research Laboratory's Life-Cycle Assessment website (EPA.gov/nrmrl/lcaccess), it's a technique for assessing the environmental aspects and potential impacts associated with a product, process, or service, by: "compiling an inventory of relevant energy and material inputs and environmental releases; evaluating the potential environmental impacts associated with identified inputs and releases; interpreting the results to help you make a more informed decision."

My problem is that they seem arbitrary; important aspects often get left out. If you're reading LCAs to help you make decisions, make sure you know who is behind the LCA (i.e., was it done by a plastic Baggie company?), and check out all of the considerations that went into the final decision. They can be helpful, but they're not infallible.

---

energy savings over waxed paper bags, provided you reused them and recycled them when possible. I don't think reusing that kind of plastic for food storage is advisable, and cannot think of any municipalities off the top of my head that recycle #4 plastic bags, which is what most zip-top sandwich bags are (not that this is written on the packages—consumers have to look it up on websites or call manufacturers to find out). Some of the energy savings can be attributed to economies of scale: More plastic bags are produced than waxed paper bags, and therefore the production is more efficient.

tip

If you're confused by a specific life-cycle assessment, see if a website like Treehugger.com has posted it online. Reader comments—informed or not—to LCAs are always enlightening.

I rarely use disposable bags or wrap. But when and if I use them, or when I have a need for something like plastic wrap (which is sometimes the must-avoid PVC #6— buyer beware), I either cover open prep bowls with a plate or a stainless steel lid, or I choose waxed paper instead. I prefer it lined with vegetable wax, not unrenewable petroleum-derived wax. Find it at IfYouCare .com or GreenFeet.com. Paper comes from a renewable resource but there are deforestation issues (I haven't run into recycled-content food-grade paper—yet), but I do reuse it, and waxed paper can biodegrade in a compost pile, while that plastic wrap and those plastic bags are swirling in the ocean, menacing marine animals.

NO MORE PAPER TOWELS!

In 2009, Greenpeace put out a report on exactly how much harm paper products do to forests and the earth (Greenpeace.org/tissue guide). It says that using 100 percent recycled content helps protect forests by reducing the demand for trees, especially trees coming from native forests. In the kitchen, cloth towels are absolutely and undeniably the way to go. If you're going to use paper towels, use the greenest version possible and only sparingly. Greenpeace ranked the following as their top products based on the fact that they contain at least 50 percent post-consumer waste and weren't bleached with chlorine, which can create the toxic by-product dioxin.

Greenpeace's top–ranking paper towel brands:
- Green Forest
- 365 Whole Planet (available at Whole Foods)
- Earth Friendly
- Natural Value
- Seventh Generation
- Trader Joe's
- Marcal Small Steps
- CVS Earth Essentials

Another great paper product resource is the Natural Resources Defense Council's Shopper's Guide to Home Tissue Products (NRDC.org/land/forests/gtissue.asp). It states that if every U.S. household replaced just one roll of virgin fiber paper towels (seventy sheets) with 100 percent recycled ones, we could save 544,000 trees. Their highest rankings go to some of the brands Greenpeace mentioned, plus Atlantic, Best Value, Earth First, Fiesta, Nature's Choice, and Pert. Notice that neither environmental nonprofit suggests buying the most well-known name brands. In fact, the NRDC specifically tells shoppers to avoid Bounty, Scott, and Viva, as they're the eco-worst. When shopping, read the fine print to find the unbleached product with the highest percentage of post-consumer waste. Just because a roll of paper towels is labeled "eco" doesn't necessarily mean a thing.

TABLETOP

Now that you've greened your pots, pans, and food storage, it's time to do the same for your dishes, glasses, utensils, and even decorations. This means using safe, environmentally friendly, and durable materials. It also means avoiding plastic and one-use-only items, like paper napkins. It does not, thankfully, mean sacrificing beauty; a conscious table is a gorgeous one.

Home Entertaining

One of the many pleasures of cooking is inviting your family and friends to share meals with you. Depending on the size of your crowd, short cuts become tempting. Resist the urge to serve on paper plates. A far better option is to use your real plates, glasses, silverware, and cloth napkins. If you won't, use only unbleached paper or compostable plates, plus unbleached or compostable paper cups and recycled-paper napkins. If using plastic cutlery, go for items made of #2, #4, or #5, especially if they can be reused and eventually recycled. If using corn or sugar plastic, make sure you can compost or recycle it where you live.

tip Most people know why to avoid lead, but many are less familiar with cadmium. It's another toxic heavy metal linked to all sorts of health issues. It's regulated by the FDA, but not in imported dishes, just like lead.

Setting the Table

Pair your plates with safe, recycled, and reusable materials. Glass is both nonreactive and can be recycled; use it for your beverages. If you're in the market for new glassware, shop around for items made from recycled glass, now available in many stores from Crate and Barrel to Green Depot. There's something amusing about

BETTER KID GEAR

DISHES

Instead of plastic (including melamine), use your own lead-free ceramic dishes, indestructible small stainless-steel prep bowls purchased at a kitchen supply store, patterned lead- and cadmium-free enamelware from Golden Rabbit (GoldenRabbit.com), and even the occasional glass bowl. I know some parents worry about shattering glass, but in my experience feeding a kid out of a practically plastic-free kitchen, breaking glass is a rare occurrence.

BIBS

Hand-me-down PVC bibs can contain lead (recent legislation means PVC and lead are less likely to be found in new ones). If you have questionable dining gear, look it up at HealthyStuff.org. For safe splashguards, place mats, and bibs, opt for natural materials. If you prefer something easy to wipe down, Mimi the Sardine's line is made from PVC-free Oeko-Tex-certified acrylic-coated organic cotton (MimiTheSardine.com). Oeko-Tex is a meaningful textile certification standard that signifies a fabric is free of a whole host of harmful substances, from carcinogenic dyes to heavy metals to formaldehyde.

UTENSILS

To avoid plastic, including spoons that change color when food is hot (who needs that?), opt for stainless-steel cocktail spoons and forks, or Bambu's kid-sized utensils made from bamboo (BambuHome.com).

SIPPY CUPS, CUPS, AND STRAWS

Metal reusable water bottle companies all make kid-sized versions. Opt for stainless steel over lined aluminum. Cups should be lead-free ceramic, lead- and cadmium-free enamelware, or glass. For straws, use stainless steel or glass—GlassDharma.com/shop or TheSoftLanding.com. People tend to wince at the idea of a glass straw, but they're thick and strong—like a Pyrex dish—and can go in the dishwasher.

LUNCH BOXES

There are a fair number of safe, PVC-free lunch sacks on the market. Mimi the Sardine makes one, and others can be found at HeroBags.com and ReusableBags.com, which also sells stainless-steel lunch boxes. So do PlanetBox.com, Lunchbots.com, and To-GoWare.com.

AVOID CRYSTAL

Crystal is glass that has been treated with lead oxide and then cut into facets. Although it is widely available from high-end companies and stores, and often passed on for generations, it's dangerous. You have to treat lead crystal beyond carefully, as almost anything can abrade it, even dust. Acid makes the lead leach into your drinks, so you cannot store anything acidic in lead crystal. This includes wine. The risk is so real that the pregnant and young are warned not to use it at all. As there are plenty of other safe and gorgeous materials to use, I just don't see the point. If you're attached to your heirlooms, just display them instead of using them.

drinking wine out of wineglasses made from recycled glass wine bottles. Or buy whatever glasses you find that strike your eye at thrift shops, garage sales, or antique stores. Lead is not an issue with glass the way it is with old dishware. Crystal is another story; buyer beware.

tip Avoid toxic-chemical-filled store-bought silver polish by scrubbing with regular old toothpaste. It works like a charm. Or, stick what you want polished in an aluminum pan, add salt and water, and presto—the tarnish will come immediately off. It's a magnetic—and magnificent—reaction.

Your utensils should ideally be durable stainless steel or silver. If you have silver, why save it for special occasions? Use it. And be sure to use cloth napkins instead of paper. Unless you're serving something really messy, it's the rare cloth napkin that needs to be laundered after every meal. Give every family member or roommate a special napkin ring, pattern, or color so they can locate theirs at the next meal. Napkins can be dish towels, cut up and hemmed old T-shirts, new organic cotton, or even hemp versions—whatever works for you. If you use a tablecloth, thrift-store finds are very green, though preferably made of natural materials. If you're shopping for a new tablecloth or napkins, opt for an eco-friendly and eco-dyed fabric.

If your table includes candles or flowers, these too should be earth and health friendly. Conventional candles tend to be made of petroleum-derived wax scented with synthetic fragrances that contain hormone disruptors, and possibly even have lead wicks. Not something you want spewing into your meals. Conventional flowers are farmed much like conventional produce: Far away and with more pesticides than you probably want to know about. Thankfully there are lovely alternatives for both. Choose to light (non-GM) soy or beeswax candles with metal-free wicks. Often you can find the latter at farmers' markets. The aroma of warm beeswax doesn't interfere with the scents of a meal or wine, but

MELAMINE

Chances are you've got something made from melamine in your kitchen, especially if you have children; most patterned kiddie bowls, plates, and cups are made from it. So are most reusable plastic items used for outdoor summer entertaining. This light, practically indestructible material seems perfect for dishware, but its production isn't eco-friendly. While it's not the same form of melamine that made its way into pet food and infant formula in recent years, sickening many and killing some, it's still a questionable choice for food because it's made with formaldehyde, which has been linked to allergies, asthma, and cancer. There's no evidence that formaldehyde leaches out of melamine every time it's used, but some studies, including one by the Danish Veterinary and Food Administration, have shown that the chemical can migrate out of melamine and into food under certain circumstances, like when in contact with acidic or hot food. It's best to avoid, especially if it is old or scratched. If you're going to use it, never ever put it in the microwave, and hand-wash it; abrasive, powdered dishwasher detergents can cause it to deteriorate. And only serve cold food or dry snacks like pretzels on it.

tip

Double-check ceramic if you're not sure it's lead-free. Call the manufacturer, and/or swab hand-me-down antique sets or anything picked up on foreign vacations with LeadCheck (see page 150). Retire anything with lead from food service. If in the market for something new, avoid buying thrift-store finds. The lead issue is too real.

if you prefer something stronger, opt for candles scented with natural essential oils, preferably organic ones. While you can find cut organic fresh flowers these days (see OrganicBouquet.com), I prefer local live plants. Other pretty alternatives include wildflowers, pinecones, gourds, and leaves in season, as well as a branch of fruit tree blossoms or a bowl of farmers' market goods.

THE LIST: DISHWARE MATERIALS
A sliding scale of choices from best to worst

- Glass (including recycled glass)
- Ceramic—lead-free only. Generally speaking, white ceramic is quite safe; patterns and colors are where lead can lurk.

AVOID: Plastic, and anything disposable, particularly for daily use

CHAPTER NINE

appliances and low-energy cooking

NUTRITIONIST AND AUTHOR JOAN GUSSOW SUGGESTED I start a revolution in these pages by telling readers *not* to buy and own every single kitchen appliance big and small. While the following pages contain information on how to choose new energy-efficient appliances, I don't actually think having all new is the way to go. So here's my revolutionary statement: Live with what you have. If something breaks, repair it. If you have to replace, do so with something energy efficient. Appliances today are often tossed when broken rather than fixed, but they aren't and shouldn't be considered disposable items. My gas stove's electric ignition recently died. Fixing it wasn't that much cheaper than buying a new (inexpensive) stove. But I didn't give in to that temptation because, as Gussow puts it, "I'm very conscious of the fact that no one magically produces chrome and steel. It's mined under hideous conditions."

Phase two of my revolution involves gadgets that no one uses daily. Why not share these? Gussow says appliance sharing was a practice that was taking off in the late 1920s and 1930s, but as our government felt that there was no economic growth in sharing, they discouraged it. Which is, I guess, how we got to our current state of stuff-driven affairs. Large-scale sharing—like a town bread oven—clearly isn't modern, but small scale can be. When I need a KitchenAid mixer, I borrow my mother's. She, in turn, borrows my immersion blender and pressure cooker. New Yorkers are stereotypically unneighborly, but I've loaned and borrowed all kinds of items to and from the people across the hall and via a local parenting community message board. People are amazingly eager to share what they get so little use out of.

tip

For more energy-saving tips for the kitchen, read *Living Like Ed: A Guide to the Eco-Friendly Life* by Ed Begley, Jr. And bookmark EnergyStar.gov, as well as the NRDC's consumer site, SimpleSteps.org.

Appliances—old, new, or shared—represent a unique opportunity to save energy. While it's tricky to calculate the energy impact of the cheese in your grilled cheese, the energy output of the toaster you used to make it is a simpler calculation. Energy-efficient appliances can save a significant amount of energy. If you're in the market for new, choose them. If you don't plan on renovating or don't have control over what fridge or stove is in your kitchen, there are still many ways to save energy with your existing appliances, plus ways to use the least amount of energy when cooking in or on any appliance.

ENERGY STAR

Surely you've seen the Energy Star tag dangling off an appliance at a store by now. Energy Star is a joint government program of the Environmental Protection Agency and the U.S. Department of Energy first introduced in 1992. It isn't perfect: In 2009, an internal audit concluded that the program doesn't properly track manufacturers using Energy Star labels. Still, it does consumers a service by certifying appliances and more—from computer monitors to air conditioners to lighting and even industrial buildings—as energy efficient through various processes. The voluntary labeling program encourages consumers and businesses to choose the best-rated products, sometimes with tax incentives. They say they have "successfully delivered energy and cost savings across the country, saving businesses, organizations, and consumers about $16 billion in 2007 alone."

Use common sense even as you rely on Energy Star. Critics of the program point out that the certification can be misleading—an energy-efficient appliance, for example, doesn't really amount to much if it is bigger than it should be, and Energy Star ratings don't factor in appliance size. It's the rare household that actually needs one of the giant refrigerators currently on the market, even if it's Energy Star rated. A small fridge will always be more efficient than a big one. *Consumer Reports* (Consumer Reports.org) says their own qualification standards are more up-to-date and stricter than those used by the Energy Star.

THE BIG APPLIANCES: FRIDGES, STOVES, AND OVENS

Refrigerators

These are the energy elephants in most kitchens. The Natural Resources Defense Council says that they account for 10 to 15 percent of the average home energy bill each month, while other groups put this estimate at 25 percent yearly. The numbers make sense—unlike other home appliances, they are on all the time. Many environmental groups suggest replacing old fridges (over ten years old) with newer, more efficient models as a way of drastically reducing energy use. New Energy Star–qualified models use 40 percent less energy than models sold even as recently as 2001. If you have an "antique" model from the seventies in your kitchen, no matter how cute it looks, a new fridge might actually consume something like 75 percent less energy. You can calculate your current fridge's energy use and compare it to newer versions on the Energy Star website (EnergyStar.gov).

While the figures on the energy calculator are make-you-want-to-shop convincing, I still haven't been able to find enough information on what exactly happens to old fridges when they get replaced. If an old unit actually gets recycled (this is not a guarantee) the refrigerants, oils, and foams, which contain ozone-depleting chemicals, might be voluntarily recovered, reclaimed, properly disposed of, or just destroyed. But doing the right thing isn't government required. The body of the fridges are usually shredded, the materials are separated, and the steel is reused for everything from cans to bridges to cars. The Energy Star site says there are more than 47 million refrigerators over ten years old in the United States—what would happen if all of them were suddenly replaced and left curbside? Energy Star's companion website, Recycle MyOldFridge.com, merely suggests asking "for assurance that the old unit will be properly recycled." That's not very concrete advice. If you're replacing a fridge, go a few steps further to ensure your unit will be truly recycled at a place that also recovers refrigerants, oils, and foams.

There are many things you can do to make the fridge you already have as efficient as possible:

tip

Bigger size usually means more energy will be consumed, but one large fridge will use less energy than two smaller ones or a smaller one plus a separate freezer. Also take configurations into account: Freezers on top or bottom use less energy than the side-by-side models.

1. Reset your thermostats. Food won't spoil and you will likely save electricity if you set your fridge between 35 and 38°F, and the freezer at 0 (some of my greenest colleagues push these numbers to 40ish for the fridge, and 5 for the freezer).

2. Clean your condenser coils, which are usually located behind or sometimes underneath your fridge. Unplug the fridge and vacuum with an attachment or use soapy warm water. Do this a few times a year if not more. By removing dust and dirt from them, you will improve air circulation and efficiency.

3. If you have the room, don't push a fridge flush against a wall. This doesn't allow air to circulate around coils located on the back. And, if you can help it, don't place it near a heat source like your oven or dishwasher, or in sunlight from a window, either. This makes it have to work harder.

RENOVATIONS

New fridge shoppers often are people doing kitchen renovations. To overgeneralize, renovations are wasteful, energy-guzzling endeavors that turn perfectly useful cabinets, sinks, and more into landfill fodder. Renovations also pollute—especially indoor air—as you go about them. Demolition releases a who-knows-what's-in-it cocktail of potentially quite harmful dust, and many of the conventional varnishes, materials, and glues used in the resulting new kitchens contain chemicals that are questionable at best. If you're eager for a change in your kitchen, try sprucing it up via cosmetic nips and tucks instead of gut renovating, or do a truly green renovation, reusing as much of what you already have as possible, and paying attention to energy use. Some good resources:

EcoHaus.com   GreenDepot.com
GreenBuilding.com   GreenGuard.org
GreenBuildingSupply.com   HealthyBuilding.net

4. Check the seal by putting a dollar in the door and shutting it. If the seal is tight, the money will stay put. If it doesn't, or if you can feel cold air coming out, you're wasting energy and need to reseal. You can buy a new seal at a hardware store. By all accounts they're not too hard to install, even if you're not handy.

5. Cool hot foods before putting them in the fridge, and don't overcrowd it.

6. A full freezer is a more energy-efficient one. Don't have enough to fill it up? Freeze some water in jugs and keep them in there; it will keep the appliance from having to work too hard. A manual defrost freezer uses half the energy of an automatic defrost one, but you have to actually defrost to keep it energy efficient.

7. If your fridge has an ice maker you don't use, turn it off to save energy.

8. If your model has a power or energy-saver switch, use it.

Stoves

When shopping for new stoves and ovens, consumers are left somewhat in the lurch, as there are currently no Energy Star labels or ratings for them (though there are for commercial ovens). Here's some basic information to help decide among gas, electric, and induction.

INDUCTION

- These use magnetic energy to produce heat and use less energy than both gas and traditional electric ranges.
- Only magnetic cookware works on them (if a magnet won't stick to your pan, it won't work on these stoves). These happen to be the safest kinds—cast iron and some stainless steel.
- They don't burn or release anything into the air you don't want to be breathing. The downside? They're pricey.

ELECTRIC

- Environmentalists will tell you that electric has advantages over natural gas, since you're not combusting anything.
- Dual-element burners help save energy—you can match the size of the burner to your pan.
- Solid-disk electric stovetops use more energy than the more common coil variety.

GAS

- Foodies swear by the quality of food cooked on a gas stove.
- It's quite energy-efficient, though natural gas is a nonrenewable resource.
- Gas stoves with electric igniters are most efficient—they use less gas (but more electricity) than ones with pilot lights. Most modern versions don't have pilot lights, unless they're commercial.

If your main stove concern is expense, keep in mind that natural gas and electricity cost different amounts in different parts of the country, and that putting in a gas line where there previously was none isn't cheap. Some people who want to use gas but don't have a line circumvent this by purchasing propane for their stove. In addition, different stoves will require different amounts of whatever energy source they use. Stoves tend to have two tags on them in stores—one is the product price, one is the operating cost. Study these.

tip

If your electric company offers electricity from clean sources like wind power, sign up for it! It may cost a little more. Make up for the expense in other ways.

Once you've considered these variables and made your stove decision, don't forget about getting an efficient hood. Thankfully, Energy Star does rate kitchen hoods. Choose one that vents fumes outside, especially for gas stoves. Buy the quietest one you can find so it won't pollute your ears, either.

MINIMIZING STOVE AND OVEN ENERGY OUTPUT

Whatever kind of cooker you have—new or old—here are ways to minimize its impact:

- Make sure all elements are in good working order.

- Match your pot size to the burner size or you will waste heat/energy.

- Pots and pans come with lids for a reason. Use them.

- If you use drip pans under your burners, keep them clean. And don't use aluminum foil liners for this purpose. Good-quality reflector pans save energy and are made to last.

- Gas stove burner holes can get clogged. If the flame is uneven or yellow, turn it off and carefully unclog it with a pin or an unfurled paper clip.

- Calibrate your oven (see page 178).

- Don't preheat, even when baking. And don't repeatedly open the oven door to check cooking items. Both waste heat. If you have an oven with a glass door, peek through there.

- Like your refrigerator, the oven door has a seal. Make sure it's tight and not sagging, and that the door hinges are in good working order.

- Don't overuse the self-cleaning feature (don't use it more than once a month), or you'll waste the energy you were hoping to save by having it. Place a sheet pan in the oven to catch drips and grease so you won't even need to clean.

- If you turn on the oven, fill it up. Use that heat to bake/roast/broil more than one thing at a time (see page 177).

- For more information, check out the following websites: American Council for an Energy Efficient Economy: ACEEE.org; Consumer EnergyCenter.org; HomeEnergy .org; EnergyStar.gov.

Ovens

Self-cleaning ovens are more efficient than non-self-cleaning ones, as they're better insulated. Still, they can contribute to indoor air pollution when doing their thing, despite the fact that you don't have to employ noxious chemicals to clean them. A tip: Use the self-cleaning option after you've cooked a meal to use the residual heat. The American Council for an Energy Efficient-Economy says convection ovens are more efficient than conventional ones. They accomplish this by circulating air to reduce cooking time.

GETTING THE MOST OUT OF YOUR OVEN

Using your big oven to make a small piece of toast is a waste of energy. When turning on your oven to make a meal, try cramming as many things as possible in it to take fullest advantage of the heat. I do this often on Sunday nights, filling it with elements of meals to last the week. Leftovers of Sunday's baked chicken with tomatoes and rosemary goes over pasta Monday, and I use the bones for stock. A roast can be dinner Sunday, leftovers Monday, and sandwich meat for a few days after that. While cooking either, I line the other racks with vegetables and more—beets can brighten salads, sweet potatoes can be turned into mash. Tomatillos can be made into salsa to go with fish or rice and beans; eggplants become babaganoush later in the week; winter squash blends quickly into a soup; and so on. You can even bake muffins at the same time. Crowding your oven to use the

tip

When oven-stuffing, keep the racks clear and don't lay foil on them. Doing so will slow down cooking time. Staggering pans improves air flow. As the oven does its Sunday night thing, put a large pot of your long-cooking grains, like brown rice, on the stovetop. Make plenty for dinner, for stirring into a soup Monday, for reheating as a stir-fry of sorts Tuesday, for coupling with beans Wednesday, and even for fashioning into garden burgers Thursday.

CALIBRATING AN OVEN

Ovens often run too hot or too cold. To fix this, you can adjust your own cooking to match however your oven seems to go, you can get a thermometer, or you can "calibrate" it (fancy lingo for fixing it). This is easiest to do with a digital stove—follow the instructions in the manual. For nondigital ovens and/or if you don't have the manual, Google the instructions for your make and model. The process can be overwhelming for the un-handy, so call in a repair person or a handy friend if needed.

heat isn't rocket science, nor is it breaking news. I've seen many variations of this oven-stuffing experiment online, and have heard of more, anecdotally, from eco-interested friends. No one has yet reported a fruit crisp that tasted like their roasted pork loin, or a bread that smacked of baked salmon. Though cookbooks tell you all of these foods need to be done at specific temperatures, all of the above do just fine at around 375°F. Keep an eye on things. If something finishes early or fast, remove it. A frittata will take less time than a giant beet, obviously. An almost-finished root vegetable will continue to cook if you kill the heat and allow it to sit in the still-hot oven. While it cools, make meringues.

tip

Reduce and reuse at the stovetop, especially with foods you make often, as it adds up. Try using less water when making pasta, and repurposing the water you boiled your beets in to, say, dye Easter eggs or color cupcake icing.

COMPARING COOKING METHODS

In general, something that doesn't take a very long time to cook uses less energy. Think about it—scrambling eggs doesn't require the time and energy that boiling eggs does (though it entails oil or butter—which have energy footprints, too). Pan searing or stovetop poaching fish is more efficient than oven baking (unless you're baking many other things at once). Broiling a chop takes less time (but is done at a higher heat) than searing it in a pan on the stove, then transferring it to the oven to finish cooking. Taste and pleasure are crucial when it comes to preparing your meals—don't force yourself to eat only scrambled if boiled is your preference. But do consider how much energy you're going to be using before you fire up the stove, just as you remember to turn off the lights when you leave a room. Make it second nature to consider energy in the kitchen and to make the most of the energy you choose to use.

Dishwashers

People really, really like to crunch numbers on washing dishes by hand versus using the machine. The going thought is that the greenest way to wash dishes is to use an Energy Star–rated dishwasher that has a built-in water-heating booster, fill it to the brim with scraped but unrinsed dishes, and choose an eco-friendly detergent. Heat boosters raise water temperature in the machine, relieving your regular hot water heater of this task, which saves energy. Turn off the machine's heated dry feature and allow dishes to air-dry

---

AT THE KITCHEN SINK

Install a faucet aerator to save water sink-side (look for how-to instructions online, or ask at the hardware store), and don't bother with the garbage disposal. TreeHugger.com reports that the garbage disposal is the worst thing that ever happened to the wastewater industry. It's much more water-and-energy-intensive work for the pipes, municipalities, and the treatment plants—greasy clogs happen, food scrap solids get trapped in screens at the plant, and much more. They were banned for many years where I live, so I know plenty of people who do perfectly fine without. Compost instead (see page 209).

to save more energy. Some machines even have an air-dry feature. There is no reason to rinse plates before putting them in, according to Ed Begley, Jr., as grinders in the exhaust drain cut up particles to prevent clogs. Read the dishwasher manual or ask the manufacturer which cycles and features on your specific model are the most efficient. If you're shopping for a new dishwasher, look inside as well as outside. Stainless-steel interiors (aka tubs) are durable, reduce noise, and retain heat for more energy-efficient drying than tubs made with other materials.

THE SMALLER APPLIANCES: MICROWAVES, TOASTER OVENS, PRESSURE COOKERS, AND MORE

Microwaves

If saving energy is your top kitchen concern, and you're not interested in a raw food diet, a microwave is your friend. Unfortunately no one with taste buds wants to eat a completely microwaved diet, but the machines have a time and a place, specifically when it comes to defrosting and warming. Of course it's not that hard or inefficient to heat up coffee on the stove, or to defrost in the fridge or water. The real savings come when you use one to drastically reduce cooking times for meals; depending on your model, a microwave uses about a third of a regular oven's energy. If you use a combination of cooking methods, you can save energy and time while still achieving the taste and texture you want. For example, stick a potato in the microwave to cook it through, then finish it in the (toaster) oven to make it crispy. In the summer, you may even save on air-conditioning costs if you microwave instead of baking.

Beyond efficiency and taste, the real issue with microwaves is their health stigma. Although this is by all accounts unfounded, it lingers—so much so that people refer to microwaving as "nuking."

According to Health Canada (sort of like our FDA), "This reference to nuclear energy is incorrect and misleading. Microwaves are a form of radiofrequency electromagnetic energy. They are generated electronically. They do not come from radioactive sources and they do not cause food or the oven itself to become radioactive." Microwaves employ, well, microwaves to penetrate food, causing water molecules in the food to rotate. The rotation causes friction that results in a quick spike in temperature. As soon as the oven shuts off, the microwaves are supposedly gone.

Still, even properly functioning microwaves that conform to government standards for emissions emit microwaves outside the unit during use. *Home Safe Home* author Debra Lynn Dadd writes on her website (DLD123.com) that home ovens emit microwaves that exceed industrial daily exposure recommendations. Health Canada states that the microwave energy that can leak from the

---

PROPER MICROWAVE MAINTENANCE

Microwave leakage will be greater if the door or seal is damaged (like if it has been dropped, or something metal exploded in the oven), or if there is a buildup of dirt around the seal. It's also important to keep hinges and latches in good working order. Some tips:

- Do not use if the door does not close or is damaged in any way.
- Follow the manufacturer's operating procedures and safety precaution instructions.
- Don't attempt repairs yourself—hire a professional.
- Do not tamper with any safety features or locks, and don't ever put anything through openings in the door seal.
- Keep the door seal and door clean, but don't use harsh cleaners that could damage them.
- For more information, check out Health Canada's site: HC-SC.GC.ca.

ovens (at levels lower than those set by international standards) has no known health risks, as long as the oven is properly maintained (see sidebar, page 181). Even if your microwave is in pristine condition, you might not want to stand in front of it as your food cooks. Yes, you're probably getting more exposure to radiation from your cordless or mobile phones, or your alarm clock if it's right next to your head all night long. But as radiation decreases with distance, I see no harm in cautiously backing up and minimizing your exposure to these emissions.

As for food safety and nutrition, Health Canada says that microwaves don't change the chemical components in food, so the formation of new compounds, like the carcinogens that arise when you char something on a grill (page 189), is unlikely. Some studies have shown that microwaved items like vegetables retain vitamins well as a result of the short cooking time. Others show microwaving decreases vitamins. All cooking methods, of course, have some effect on nutrients, and it's well known that the longer you cook something, the less nutrients it retains. That said, most of us don't cook in only one way. If you're really concerned about losing nutrients when you cook your food in a microwave or anywhere else, vary your cooking methods and throw some extra raw goods into your next salad.

What's the takeaway here? If you have a microwave and you like using it, or if you're an energy savings junkie who cannot walk

tip
To save the most energy in a kitchen, cook as often as possible in a combination of countertop toaster oven, microwave, and pressure cooker. Home electronics use energy even when off, so plug them all into power strips, and flip the switch to truly turn them off when not in use. Or just pull the plugs out of the wall sockets. When it comes to using the oven, do so minimally—remember that stovetop burners use less energy than the oven itself.

WHAT TO MICROWAVE IN?

Guess what? "Microwave-safe" is not a third-party-certified or government-regulated claim. It infers that the material—be it ceramic or plastic or glass—does not absorb the microwaves and therefore heats up very slowly and that it won't leach its chemicals into your food. But studies, including an investigation by the *Milwaulkee Journal Sentinel*, have found high levels of BPA released from heated containers marked "microwave safe." Despite the lack of regulation of this term, items that are labeled "microwave-safe" are, oddly, according to the FDA and the American Plastics Council, the only plastic that should be used in a microwave. Environmental health experts, on the other hand, do not recommend putting *any* plastic in the microwave, even "microwave-safe" plastic. I agree. Use glass, or use no container at all when cooking root vegetables if the turntable in your microwave is made of glass. Carryout containers from restaurants, old cream cheese tubs, Styrofoam, or any plastic container made specifically to hold cold food should never, ever be used in a microwave, as they're specifically known to leach their chemical components into food when heated. Discard containers that hold prepared microwaveable or other convenience meals after one use, as they're only meant for that one use. If you're going to use "microwave-safe" plastic wrap, the experts agree it should not directly touch your food; read the labels on packaging for instructions. And do not reuse wrap that came with, say, your cheese as a cover in the microwave, as there is no way of knowing what it's made of. For more information, see the USDA Food Safety Inspection Service's microwave ovens and food safety fact sheets: www.FSIS.USDA.gov. If you have any doubt about whether something is safe to put in a microwave, *don't put it in the microwave.* Go back to your cabinet and find something that clearly is microwaveable.

away from such a low-impact machine, make sure it's in good condition. Keep in mind that *Consumer Reports* says more research is needed with regard to certain aspects of microwave safety, so do proceed with caution. If shopping for a microwave, used ones are not a good idea.

MICRO CUISINE

Microwaving your grass-fed steak isn't a way to honor the protein or your taste buds, despite the efficiency of the machine. Some sacrifices should not be made! If you're going to employ the microwave for more than defrosting, reheating, and pre-"baking" potatoes and would like to avoid making rubbery mistakes with hotspots, invest in a copy of *Microwave Gourmet* by Barbara Kafka.

Jonathan Zearfoss, a professor at the Culinary Institute of America, swears by "poaching" eggs in the microwave (crack an egg into a small glass prep bowl or "microwave-safe" ceramic ramekin, zap for forty-five seconds to one minute). I tested his handy-when-it-works recipe and the results varied, even in the same bowl in the same microwave. I guess no two eggs are alike. Some even blow up before that forty-five-second mark. It can be a fun experiment, but messy. The result is tasty, if a bit too chewy, and not as soft or good as stovetop poached.

Toaster Ovens

One potato in a giant oven is a waste of energy. Enter the toaster oven. It may not be practical for family meals, but if you're cooking for one, you might use it more than your big oven. A new toaster oven may be more efficient than an older one, but don't write off what you already have in your home, for several reasons. First, the interior of pretty much every countertop toaster for sale today is lined with a questionable nonstick coating (see page 146). Manufacturers say it's for the ease of cleaning, but I've never found wiping crumbs hard enough to warrant the chance of nonstick chemicals entering my cheese melt. Older models might not have such linings. Call the manufacturer to find out if yours does.

Another reason to use what you already have is just that: You already have it and it works. Don't toss it. Toasters—and many other small appliances—aren't even currently Energy Star certifiable. Whatever countertop version you already have uses less energy than a real oven so the savings are built-in. If you have only a slot toaster and are looking to replace it with a more versatile toaster oven, that's a different story.

Pressure Cookers

Northeastern turnips and rutabagas can grow as big as my cat's head come Halloween. If you try to bake one of these whole, you'll have the oven on for hours. But stick it in a pressure cooker, follow the manufacturer's basic instructions, and—like an infomercial miracle—it will be done in mere minutes. Try it for dried soaked beans and rice, too. This sure beats beans from a can containing bisphenol-A, or spending hours cooking dried beans on the stovetop. Pressure-cooking chicken (brown it first) can easily take thirty-plus minutes less than stovetop stewing. Beef stew? Hours less! And, unlike microwave cooking, pressure cooker cooking is, across the board, really quite flavorful and good. It takes some experimenting to get it right, and there are plenty of pressure cooker cookbooks and even YouTube videos that can serve as guides. Make sure your pressure cooker is stainless steel and not lined with nonstick coating, and buy a size that makes sense for you—the most common size is 6 quarts. Don't worry about the top blowing off; today's pressure cookers are better-designed than those of yore.

OTHER APPLIANCES

For all other gadgets in the kitchen, follow some general shopping rules.

1. "Shop" your own kitchen—chances are you already have everything you need. And then some. If you decide you really need something new, check around with friends and family to see if anyone has what you want that they might

want to offload. If not, do some research to find the greenest, most efficient version of whatever you're looking for. Keep in mind that this might mean not buying the cheapest blender, coffeemaker, or mixer available. You want something durable that comes with a warrantee. Double up wherever you can—a Crock-Pot can do one-pot meals as well as rice, eliminating the need for a rice cooker.

2.   Look at the materials. The part of any gadget that touches your food should be made of safe and durable materials. A glass blender is preferable to a plastic one. Stainless steel is preferable to aluminum, which is preferable to something lined with a nonstick surface. Ceramic Crock-Pot linings should be lead-free. Find out if the item you're seeking is safe to buy secondhand—George Foreman–type grills, sandwich presses, and waffle irons are often nonstick, and therefore could be too scratched and iffy to buy used.

3.   Is there a nonelectric version of what you need? Small appliances don't use enough energy to really fret about, but using many of them does add up. Certain antique hand juicers (the ones with pull levers) squeeze with the same amount of elbow grease as electric citrus juicers, and appear to yield even more juice. Reamers or even forks also work well for citrus. Do you really need an electric knife sharpener, or can you master a DIY steel? Pay extra attention to the appliances you use daily—can you replace a coffeemaker with a hand-press carafe and still love your morning brew?

GRILLING

No one can deny the allure of an open fire. Cooking outside makes sense when the weather is warm, but there are a number of things to scrutinize before you grill. Foodies have long debated the merits of charcoal versus gas. Gas, a nonrenewable resource, is a convenient and controllable way to cook on an open flame, but where taste is concerned, charcoal always wins. Environmentally speaking, though, charcoal is worse than gas. Among other negatives, charcoal promotes deforestation (it is made from trees) and pollutes the air as it burns. This

tip

There are hybrid grills on the market that allow you to use a bit of wood or charcoal for flavor and either gas or electric as the main power source. Best of both worlds.

might not seem like a big deal if you're the sort who grills once in a blue moon, but think about how much pollution gets collectively released into the air on a day like July 4. According to an article in the July/August 2005 issue of *Sierra* magazine, an estimated sixty million barbecues are held on this holiday, during which Americans burn the equivalent of 2,300 acres of forest and release 225,000 metric tons of carbon dioxide into the air. Research has shown that in areas where people grill often, fatty acids in meat smoke can contribute to hazy skies. Fat smog! If you aren't prepared to give up grilling, it's good to be aware of the impact it can have on both your health and the environment and to minimize it however you can.

Here's a roundup of all the basic environmental concerns regarding the different ways to grill, as well as advice on how to be more efficient with your method of choice.

Gas Grills

Opting for gas means avoiding the pollution and health risks associated with lighter fluid and charcoal smoke. Propane is found mixed with natural gas and oil and is separated out at natural gas processing plants and crude oil refineries. It's fairly clean-burning but is a nonrenewable fossil fuel that emits CO_2. Still, gas barbecues produce about half as much CO_2 as charcoal grills, and about a third as much as electric grills, making them the unexpectedly efficient winner in this category. Natural gas burns even cleaner than propane, so a natural gas grill (which connects to the gas line in your house as opposed to a tank) is worth considering. High BTUs do equal energy waste, so keep that in mind when shopping for a quality, durable grill.

Electric Grills

Electric grills are the second-most-energy-efficient traditional grilling option. They use less BTUs per hour than gas grills and save on crude oil use, especially if you get your electricity from an alternative source like wind power. According to The Daily Green (TheDailyGreen.com), they emit 99 percent less carbon monoxide than charcoal grills. The actual grilling is similar to using a propane grill. If you don't have electrical sockets outside, consider having them installed.

THE LIST: GRILLS
A sliding scale of choices from best to worst

- Solar cookers (not technically grills) cook outside using nothing but the sun's energy
- Electric, natural gas, and propane: they burn cleaner and are more efficient than charcoal or wood
- Hybrid grills, using as little natural charcoal or wood as possible
- Natural charcoal and hard wood, using a chimney starter

AVOID: Conventional charcoal, charcoal containing lighter fluid, and lighter fluid in general

CHARRING

High-heat techniques like grilling can produce carcinogens. To reduce the risk, avoid the char. Here's how:

- Trim meats of fat that can cause charring flare-ups.
- Lean meats cooked over indirect heat, away from hot coals (if you're using them), are less likely to flare.
- Marinades with citrus juices, olive oil, and herbs are said to help keep char from forming on food.
- Choosing gas over charcoal helps you avoid eating soot.
- If you have char, cut or scrape the blackened parts off before eating.

Charcoal Grills

Charcoal produces the best grill flavor, but there's no such thing as 100 percent eco-friendly briquettes or lump charcoal, and burning either of them pollutes. Conventional charcoal briquettes are made from sawdust, which has residues of coal dust, sodium nitrate, and other things you don't want to release into the air (soot, carbon monoxide) or onto your food. Hardwood lump charcoal is preferable as it doesn't contain these undesirables, but its production contributes to deforestation and global warming.

Avoid easy-light lumps like the plague: They have been soaked in lighter fluid, which gives off several nasty volatile organic compounds (VOCs—"organic" in this context has nothing to do with USDA organic) while burning, a smell most of us are quite familiar with and not something you want to be breathing. A much better option is to use a newer alternative to conventional charcoal, especially one made from invasive tree species or environmentally certified wood (like those given the stamp by the Forest Stewardship Council or certified by the Rainforest Alliance's SmartWood

SHANNON HAYES'S PERFECT-EVERY-TIME STEAK (GRASSFEDCOOKING.COM)

Grass-fed meat is sometimes leaner, more variable, and can have more pronounced muscle tissue (and fuller flavor), so it needs to be grilled differently from conventional meat. "What matters is how you handle the fire and the meat," says Shannon Hayes, author of *The Farmer and the Grill, The Grassfed Gourmet Cookbook,* and *Radical Homemakers.* She works with her family on Sap Bush Hollow Farm in upstate New York. "Whether you're cooking filet mignon, top loin, rib-eye, T-bone, or porterhouse, the basic method is the same." If steaks are boneless, allow one half pound per person; for bone-in, allow one pound per person.

Serves 2 to 4 (boneless) or 1 to 2 (bone-in),
depending on size of steak

1 to 2 tablespoons coarse salt, depending on size of steak

2 to 3 teaspoons freshly ground black pepper, depending on size of steak

2 cloves garlic, minced

program), and clean-burning ones made from other plant materials. Bonus: Unlike gas, these are renewable resources. Though not yet the sort of thing you can find at every beach town gas station, places like co-ops, natural food stores, and bigger chains like Whole Foods do tend to stock at least one eco-friendlier brand in warmer months. They can also easily be found online—

1 to 2 pounds of any of the following: 1 sirloin, sirloin tip, tri-tip, top round, or London broil steak; or 2 shoulder top blade, shoulder petite tender, rib, porterhouse, T-bone, top loin (aka NY strip), or tenderloin (aka filet mignon) steaks, about $1\frac{1}{2}$ inches thick

1. Combine the salt, pepper, and garlic in a small bowl. Rub the mixture into both sides of the steak, then allow the meat to come to room temperature while you prepare the grill.

2. Preheat the grill to medium-hot. If you are using a gas grill, turn off all but one of the burners once it has come up to temperature. If you are using charcoal, be sure all of the coals have been raked to one side. Using the hand test, the grate will be hot enough when you can hold your palm five inches above the metal for no more than three seconds.

3. Sear the steaks for 3 minutes on each side directly over the flame, with the lid down. Then, move the steaks to the part of the grill that is not lit. Lower the lid and allow the steaks to cook, without flipping them, until they reach 120 to 140°F, 15 to 25 minutes, depending on the size of the steak. Remove the steaks to a platter, and serve. Because the cooking is indirect, the juices don't need recovery time to redistribute.

Char-Broil Hickory Wood Chunks uses FSC-certified wood and is available on Amazon.com. Check out the coconut shell briquettes from GreenlinkCharcoal.com. Big-box stores like Home Depot and Wal-Mart do sell the pure lump charcoal with no additives from various kinds of woods. They may not be FSC-certified, but are preferable to conventional lumps. Look for them.

Smoking

If you like smoke in your 'cue—no matter which kind of grill you're using—keep in mind that harvesting wood can contribute to deforestation, and grilling with it releases ash and smoke. Consider slow-burning hardwoods, like fast-growing mesquite, kiawe, and hickory, over pine and other fast-burning softwoods; you'll burn less of them. If you have access to wood you particularly trust, burn that. Chef and author Deborah Madison mainly uses a propane grill, but she also has a small Weber she fills with prunings from her own apple trees.

Solar Ovens

Though impractical for an evening cookout, solar cookers are an environmentally perfect option for an outdoor party, even in the winter. It's basically a solar crock pot, not a grill. Put the food in and leave it alone until it's done. The results will be stewlike. It's slow going but avoids emissions entirely, and cooking without a flame eliminates the health concerns regarding charred food (see sidebar, page 189). For more information on cooking outside without using electricity, propane, or fossil fuels, surf over to the Solar Oven Society (SolarOven.org). Beware of overcast weather unless you have a hybrid solar oven, which has an electric backup element (EarthEasy.com).

tip

When faced with the prospect of greasy, marinade-sticky pans, aluminum foil seems like a cook's gift. Environmentally speaking, it's resource-intensive to make. Make do without. If you like to "tent" your meat with foil after it comes off the grill, try using a dishcloth. If you're going to use foil, look for recycled foil. Clean and recycle it after use, if your local center accepts it. It's highly recyclable stuff. According to Grist.org's eco-advice columnist, Umbra Fisk, "Americans are said to throw away enough aluminum in three months to rebuild our entire commercial air fleet." Ack.

ENTERTAINING

When inviting people over for a barbecue party, don't skimp on ingredients. If grass-fed meat for twenty is out of your budget, go veggie, or mainly veggie. Or throw a potluck party. If cash isn't of concern and you want someone else to do the grilling for you, hire a green-leaning caterer well versed in everything from conventional meat to bleached tablecloths. Mary Cleaver of the Cleaver Company (CleaverCo.com) has been catering for over a quarter of a century and seamlessly weaves ecological touches into every aspect of her sustainable company—carefully sourcing the tastiest small farm ingredients, (politely) getting guests to reuse their glasses, and composting everything possible post-party. You can always dictate that your caterer do the same, but it's easiest to work with someone eco-knowledgeable. To find eco-leaning caterers near you, Cleaver suggests looking on ChefsCollaborative.com for sustainable caterers or members who could make informed referrals.

Post-Party

Take care to dispose of all grilling detritus in the least harmful manner. Recycle and compost what you can. Wood ash can be used like fertilizer in a garden, but conventional charcoal ash will contain residues of the chemicals it contained, so keep it out of your garden, and especially away from a vegetable garden. It can harm the plants as well as you and it belongs in the garbage. Next, wipe off the grill and any outdoor furniture with green cleaners (chapter ten). Prep pans and other dishes should be washed in eco-friendly soap. No one wants ammonia or chlorine bleach residue on their next Certified Humane burger.

cleanup

A CONSCIOUS KITCHEN GETS AS MESSY AS ANY OTHER kitchen. It's a space that should be cleaned with eco- and people-friendly cleaning products and reusable rags instead of harsh cleaners and paper towels, as well as protected by nontoxic pest management to discourage the bugs and vermin that like kitchens as much as humans do.

CLEANING PRODUCTS

Changing your conventional cleaning products to green versions—today—is a simple and effective way to drastically reduce your indoor air pollution and your environmental impact. Back in the day, some green cleaners weren't as effective as their conventional counterparts, and the good ones were often hard to find. But now there's no excuse for not using green cleaners. They're extremely effective, widely available, don't cost extra, and come from many manufacturers—even from the cleaning product giants that produce the most toxic conventional versions. If you're not already cleaning with ecologically sound products and are skeptical, take the first step by swapping out the one conventional product you use the most (bleach? glass cleaner?) with its green counterpart. I promise you won't miss the carcinogens, hormone disrupters, or lung, eye, and throat irritants.

Some eco-scrubs and sprays are greener than others, and a few claim to be green when they're not. Do a little research before shopping—knowing to read ingredient labels in-store isn't always enough when it comes to buying cleaning products. Oddly, cleaning product formulations are protected by the government as trade secrets, so companies do not have to disclose their product ingredients. But truly green brands willingly list their ingredients on their bottles, and go even further in explaining their formulations on their websites. Environmental groups have been trying to encourage all companies to disclose their ingredients. You should largely be able to understand the voluntarily listed ingredients. If you can't, buy something else (see sidebar, page 200).

Lacking ingredient lists, you can study and become an expert on the heady mix of petroleum-derived carcinogens, indoor air pollutants, and endocrine disrupters in most conventional products (see "Cheat Sheet," page 198). You can learn all there is to know about the harmful effects of various kinds of bleaches—from manufacture to disposal. You can research every report you can find about surfactants, and the carcinogenic by-products lingering in some dish soaps. You can play citizen scientist/sleuth in an effort to figure out whom you trust— environmental groups or cleaning product manufacturers and the groups they support. You can get to the bottom of what the manufacture and use of optical brighteners really does to fish (it's not pretty) and what the benzene in your oven cleaner means for you and the environment. You can try to remember which of these chemicals react if mixed together to form

tip

Open your windows. Ventilation is the key to healthy indoor air. Even in winter. Even in cities.

CLEANING PRODUCT MANUFACTURERS IN COURT

In 2009, Earthjustice (Earthjustice.org) and other nonprofit groups took Procter & Gamble, Colgate-Palmolive, "and other household cleaner manufacturing giants to court for refusing to follow a New York State law requiring them to disclose the chemical ingredients in their products and the health risks they pose." They say the long-ignored law from 1976 "requires household cleaner companies selling their products in New York to file semi-annual reports with the state listing the chemicals contained in their products and describing any company research on these chemicals' health and environmental effects." SC Johnson was not targeted in the lawsuit because "after receiving notice last fall from Earthjustice that it was out of compliance with the state law, the company began a dialogue with Earthjustice and other groups about how it might come into compliance." As a result, they've begun to disclose their ingredients on product labels and via WhatsInside SCJohnson.com. Other industry giants have pledged to follow suit in 2010. Here's hoping much more will come out of this ongoing and groundbreaking lawsuit. Check Earthjustice's website for the most up-to-date information.

---

even worse inhalation hazards (hint: ammonia and bleach). You can attempt to figure out how long residues last on surfaces and what's truly safe to use around food. You can then do guesswork to decipher which cleaning products contain these chemicals in an effort to avoid taking them home. The information is out there. Or you can go green. It's so much easier, less confusing, and better for you and the environment. It's just really common sense.

Keep in mind that the purest green products won't make your house smell like anything much. Natural scent does not linger in the air. That said, some eco-friendlier products are being made with synthetic fragrances that do linger. Most of the environmentally concerned brands that use synthetic fragrances (Mrs. Meyers and Method come to mind) say they use phthalate-free scents and are forthcoming about them. Purists contend that green products shouldn't contain these synthetics at all. But an environmentally friendly product containing what Mrs. Meyers refers to as a "safe synthetic" is still preferable to any conventional counterpart. I opt for natural.

Disinfecting

Home kitchens get dirty, but this doesn't mean they need over-the-top disinfecting. Even where raw meat juice and spilled garbage are concerned, something as harsh as bleach just isn't called for. For most cleanup, the strongest cleaner needed is hot soapy water and elbow grease, or a mixture of water and vinegar. To kill the worst bacteria that might be lurking in a kitchen, a peroxide-based cleaner will do. Most green brands make them and label them "kitchen cleaner." Just read the bottle to see if a green product contains peroxide. Don't believe it's strong enough? Eco and people-friendly hydrogen peroxide is registered by the EPA as an antimicrobial pesticide. There are hospitals now using industrial green hydrogen-peroxide-based cleaners instead of conventional bleach-based ones. I'd argue that hospitals are concerned with killing off a lot worse germs that you've got swarming on your butcher block. Some people are very partial to their bleach, despite the health and environmental concerns. If you're one of them, read and follow the instructions on the bottle; the amount of bleach the average person uses at home tends to be way above what is actually needed. You're only supposed to use a small amount and dilute it. Bleach users and users of other conventional cleaning products should also be very careful with where they store it, especially if there are curious kids or pets at home. Same goes for green cleaners. No one should be drinking bottles of them, but in the scheme of things, they're less of a risk.

tip

When choosing between green products, factor in the packaging. Look for ultraconcentrated multi-purpose cleaners that come in bottles made with post-consumer-content recycled plastic. Dilute to varying degrees for different jobs.

CHEAT SHEET

The following are what personal and environmental health journalist Mindy Pennybacker (GreenerPenny.com), former editor-in-chief of the Green Guide, referred to as some of the worst cleaning product ingredients in an article from March 2006. You won't likely find them listed on any bottle, so the only way to avoid them is to never buy conventional products. For more information, go to GreenerChoices.org/ecolabels.

- **Alkylphenol ethoxylates (APEs),** common in detergents and disinfectants, are suspected hormone disruptors.

- **Ammonia** is poisonous when swallowed, extremely irritating to respiratory passages when inhaled, and can burn the skin on contact.

- **Antibacterial cleansers containing triclosan** may be contributing to the rise of antibiotic-resistant germs.

- **Butyl cellosolve (aka butyl glycol, ethylene glycol monobutyl)** is poisonous when swallowed and is a lung-tissue irritant.

- **Chlorine bleach (aka sodium hypochlorite),** an all-purpose whitening agent, can irritate the lungs and eyes, and in waterways can become toxic organochlorines.

- **Diethanolamine (DEA)** can combine with **nitrosomes** (often-undisclosed preservatives) to produce carcinogenic nitrosamines that penetrate skin.

- **Fragrance** frequently contains **phthalates,** chemicals linked to reproductive abnormalities and liver cancer in lab animals, and to asthma in children.

- **Phosphates** soften water for detergents but contribute to algae blooms in our waterways, which can kill off fish populations.

- **Sodium hydroxide**—found in drain, metal, and oven cleaners—is extremely irritating to eyes, nose, and throat and can burn those tissues on contact.

- **Sodium lauryl sulfate,** a common sudsing agent, can penetrate the skin and cause contact dermatitis.

HOW HAZARDOUS IS SOMETHING, REALLY?

If you wonder what to do when there is no ingredient list on a specific product—like those bleach wipes your child's preschool teachers drag across the table just before snack—try Googling the name of it and "MSDS." MSDS stands for "material safety data sheet." These are government-required forms for all potentially hazardous materials or material mixes that contain data regarding the properties of certain substances. They're a little tough to read, as they aren't made for consumers; they're designed for workplace protection, meant to safeguard emergency responders or workers exposed to these substances on a daily basis. I find it particularly enlightening to read the health effect information portion of MSDS sheets, but keep in mind that my (or your) in-home exposure level is nowhere near that of someone working in, say, a cleaning product manufacturing plant. Consumers can access the product-specific sheets on manufacturer websites or via any number of online MSDS databases.

DIY Cleaners

There are very few cleaners you can't make yourself at home with some mix of water, vinegar, baking soda, and eco-friendly liquid or dish soap. They're inexpensive, easy, and effective.

- Soap plus water equals mopping solution.
- Soap plus baking soda and a drop or two of water equals excellent mildly abrasive scouring paste. Extras to mix in include lemon, natural essential oils, or even hydrogen peroxide.
- Water plus vinegar equals glass cleaner.

For other cleaning product recipes (and much more), I defer to the excellent reference books *Better Basics for the Home: Simple Solutions for Less Toxic Living* and *Clean and Green: The Complete Guide to Non-Toxic and Environmentally Safe Housekeeping*, both by Annie Berthold-Bond.

GREEN CLEANING PRODUCTS

Here are some of the purest brands for everything from dish soap and detergent to glass cleaner to all-purpose sprays. Some are more widely available than others. Knock yourself out.

Vermont Soap Organics, VermontSoap.com
Dr. Bronner's, DrBronner.com
Ecover, Ecover.com
Seventh Generation, SeventhGeneration.com
Biokleen, BiokleenHome.com

Wipes

Beyond your chosen cleaner, it's important to green what you're wiping counters and stovetop with. This is a great opportunity to reuse old washcloths, T-shirts that are past their wearable life, and the like. If you're addicted to paper towels, there's no time like the present to kick the habit. In the interim, buy only unbleached recycled versions (see page 162), and see how long you can make one roll last. As for sponges, there are currently plenty on the market claiming to be natural. Try them and see how they work for you. I was very fond of a wonderfully packaged and marketed biodegradable, petrochemical-free, undyed natural sponge with a loofah scrubby side until, while researching this book, I noticed that the material comes from Norway and is manufactured in China before arriving at my local store (how's that for carbon footprint?). It's also treated with an antibacterial agent. When shopping for natural-colored sponges, read the fine print to avoid ones containing antimicrobial pesticides. Most have them and are labeled accordingly. Whatever sponges you use, store them in dry

> **tip**
> Use a vacuum cleaner with a HEPA filter— they trap the smallest dust particles. This is important, as chemical residues cling to dust.

places between use, and disinfect them—especially after working with raw meat—by boiling them for three minutes or popping them, damp, in the microwave for a minute. A slightly less effective way to disinfect is to run them through the dishwasher. When sponges have gone past their useful kitchen life, they can still be used to clean floors or for dirty outdoor jobs.

PESTS

Treat your home with an integrated pest management system (see page 18) similar to what your local orchards might have in place. The first thing to do is to prevent pests and bug infestations before they happen. If you have no bugs or mice currently in your kitchen, do not gloss over this section! You never know when they might pay a visit. And you're more likely to have to use a pesticide once they arrive. Prevention is crucial.

Start by making sure there is no way for creatures to enter your kitchen by sealing up holes in your walls with no-VOC caulk (you can buy it at GreenDepot.com) and/or steel wool. Next, keep your kitchen clean. Don't invite unwanted guests in with crumbs and other treats. Finally, if and when there is an infestation, treat it as nontoxically as possible. Maybe the spring ants that come every year don't bother you much and can be dissuaded from taking over with a little borax-sugar-water solution. (Similar treatments for other critters

tip To find eco-friendly pest busters, and those practicing IPM near you, check out GreenShieldCertified .org. Operated by the IPM Institute of North America, recognized by the EPA, and advised by many experts, including one from the NRDC, Green Shield is a meaningful, independent certification. One caveat: Keep some of that no-VOC caulk on hand; it's the rare IPM practitioner that considers what's in the caulk they're filling your wall holes with.

can be found on the very helpful Least Toxic Control of Pests in the Home and Garden list at BeyondPesticides.org; click on alternatives fact sheets.) These alternatives are much better for you and the earth than bombing your home with caustic fumes. Roaches may require something stronger, but call in a green pesticide expert only when needed. If you live in a building where the management decides who exterminates in your apartment, you can refuse to let them enter your home and pay for your own exterminator of choice if you need one. Or ask the management to switch over to a company that uses less harsh chemicals. If they're reluctant, hand them a copy of the EPA study *American Healthy Homes Survey: A National Study of Residential Pesticides Measured From Floor Wipes*, which demonstrates that pesticides can linger in kitchens years after they're applied, including ones that have been banned in this country for decades. Whatever you use now will be better for the future inhabitants of your space, too.

CHAPTER ELEVEN

waste

EVERYTHING WE CONSUME CREATES SOME AMOUNT OF WASTE. Industrial sources may contribute more to the landfills than individuals, but our collective toss-outs create quite the methane-producing landfill pileup, especially when you factor in food packaging, discarded gadgets, and broken appliances. All too often people who are just starting to go green feel like they're already doing enough with their garbage by recycling it. We do need to recycle. But remember the order of the three Rs. There's a reason Reduce and Reuse come *before* Recycle. When standing in front of your garbage, the choice shouldn't only be recycle or throw away. There's no such thing as "away." It's just elsewhere. Collectively reducing and reusing (which often involves repairing) are how we're truly going to impact what's happening in our landfills. Recycling alone isn't enough.

REDUCE AND REUSE FIRST

One great place to start to move away from the recycle-or-trash way of thinking about garbage is to think about waste when you're shopping. Buy grains, lentils, nuts, dried fruit, cereal, and

A YEAR OF GARBAGE

There have been a number of Internet sites of late devoted to peple saving their trash for a period of time, the most notable being regular-guy-cum-eco-hero Dave Chameides's undertaking. He saved his for a full year (2008) in his Los Angeles basement (see his endeavor and ensuing journey at 365daysoftrash.blogspot.com). Recording the process is like waste performance art—when you show the world the enormity of what you're throwing out, it makes others stop and think about how to cut down their own giant loads. As a result of the experience, Chameides reduced his yearly trash output to what an average family tosses in one week. Check out his tips on how to follow in his footsteps on his blog. Though saving garbage for a year is extreme, and possibly off-putting to some, his suggestions are not. They're sensible, simple approaches that everyone and anyone can apply in their homes.

tip **Landfills are the biggest source of anthropogenic (man-made) methane emissions in the United States.** Methane, a potent greenhouse gas, is made when biodegradable items like food waste, yard waste, and paper decompose without oxygen (see page 209). How can you help? Recycle and start composting.

whatever else you can find in bulk and in reusable containers, like cotton produce bags (see page 160). If bulk items aren't available where you shop, opt for items that come in the least amount of packaging. Can you buy milk and beer in returnable glass bottles? If your cereal comes in a box with a plastic bag inside, can you buy one just in plastic? Avoid individually wrapped single-serve items, too, like kiddie yogurts and cheese slices. Buy larger sizes, and slice your own blocks of cheese to cut down on all the packaging waste.

Another thing to look for is packaging that contains some recycled content. Food doesn't often come in post-consumer-content material, but sometimes it does, and dish soaps and kitchen cleaners certainly do, especially the eco brands. Recycled materials save energy, pollute less, and reduce the use of trees, fossil fuels, and minerals. Voting with your dollars and choosing recycled packaging also signals to manufacturers that such products are in demand.

It's a nice bit of synergy that if you eat the whole foods and drink the drinks described throughout these pages, you will largely have less to throw out. Avoid junk and packaged processed food and there will be less packaging to reuse, recycle, or toss. Don't buy bottled water or other beverages (see page 96) and you won't be contending with those bottles. CSA and farmers' market produce is either un- or minimally packaged. Buy your grass-fed meat wrapped in paper from a butcher rather than getting it shrouded in plastic at the supermarket. "The more I follow my nose about local food the less I have to worry about that," says author and locavore Barbara Kingsolver. "There are no cans in my pantry. The devils we know seem to mostly go away when we begin to simplify and localize our system."

THE THIRD R: RECYCLING

Have you ever truly considered or even tried to research what, exactly, happens after you put that plastic water bottle in a municipal recycling bin? On the most basic level, the best-case scenario is that it goes off to a well-run recycling center near where you live (to find one, go to Earth911.com), and it gets broken down—with minimal chemicals and fumes—into something usable. But the original bottle won't ever be 100 percent reusable, as most people assume it is. The plastic is usually downgraded, which means that the bottle won't become a new bottle post-recycling, but will be something else, or part of something else. Inevitably some portion of the plastic water bottle will end up as waste. And the chemicals and methods used to break plastic items down, like the chemicals and methods used to build them in the first place, are environmentally harsh. Worst-case scenario, the bottle you spent a few hours or minutes drinking from and then mindfully recycled gets tossed in the land-fill, where it will sit for long after your life-time, or it's shipped off to a faraway land like China and burned in an open incin-erator to break it down. Unfathomable but true that we ship some of our garbage to other countries that are willing to take it. Burning plastic—especially out in the open—is a serious health risk for the work-ers charged with this task, for their fami-lies, and for the earth.

tip

Before shopping, familiarize yourself with what's recycled in your area. Despite the arrow symbols on the bottom of most plastic packaging that lead the masses to think other-wise, not everything is recyclable. Well, theoretically it is, but your town might not recycle it. On a card, write down the basic numbers and shapes of the plastic packaging your town does recycle. Stick the list in your wallet to guide you as you shop. Choose the items you want that come in those materials.

In New York, the city government maintains a long, tidy explanation on its website of what happens to the recyclables in citizens' bins. In 2009, the site stated that between 366,000 and 423,000 tons per year of mixed paper recyclables and between 250,000 and 331,000 tons per year of metal, glass, and plastic recyclables are delivered to "private processors." The site provides a list of the private processors for paper, and men-tions the one processor for metal, glass, and plastic. And it states that barges are used to transport both kinds of recyclables to where they get processed in order to minimize trucking. The transparency implied by this information is comforting, but I still don't entirely understand what happens to my recyclables or to the many yogurt cups and the like that New Yorkers attempt to recycle but that the city of New York doesn't recycle.

What to Do with Recyclables Your Municipality Doesn't Recycle

Despite plastic bags' newfound terrible reputation, they can actually be recycled, though not many places do this. Those plastic bags stashed under the kitchen sink can either be reused again and again, or brought to someone who does recycle them. New York City, which has yet to enact an all-out ban on plastic bags, requires larger retail and chain stores to accept clean plastic bags for recycling. So while residents can't toss them into the recycling bins the city picks up, they can walk them over to their local chain stores and drop them off in clearly marked containers. In 2009, when this law was put in place, the city said plastic bags alone comprised about 2.87 percent of New York City's residential waste stream, which makes them the largest source of plastic in NYC's waste. Similar programs can be found in other cities and states and are worth seeking out. It's minimal consumer effort, especially when you consider how much plastic is floating around in the middle of the ocean or stuck not biodegrading in landfills.

When it comes to broken appliances, try to repair before tossing. All too often we assume a broken item is dead for good, when it's something our parents would have

tip

If you eat lunch daily at an office, you might be alarmed by the amount of trash you produce. Reduce it by stashing nonplastic real tableware in your desk. Pack your own lunch, or if you don't, Dave Chameides suggests carrying a reusable, collapsible bowl in your bag so you won't resort to taking and tossing plastic clamshells day in and day out. You can just hand it to the person behind the takeout counter to fill with your order. Yes, it's also plastic, but it's a great alternative to the other plastic you'd use for mere minutes that then lasts a lifetime in the landfill.

FIVE STRATEGIES TO REDUCE THE ENVIRONMENTAL IMPACT OF PLASTICS

The Ecology Center (EcologyCenter.org), a Berkeley, California–based organization devoted to educating and training the public about sustainable living, offers up five solid ways to reduce the eco-impact of plastic. They're uniquely qualified to give this advice as they also run Berkeley's residential curbside recycling program, plastic-bag-free farmers' markets, and more.

1. **Reduce the use.** Retailers and consumers can select products that use little or no packaging. Select packaging materials that are recycled into new packaging—such as glass and paper. If people refuse plastic as a packaging material, the industry will decrease production for that purpose, and the associated problems such as energy use, pollution, and adverse health effects will diminish.

2. **Reuse containers.** Since refillable plastic containers can be reused about twenty-five times [preferably not for food], container reuse can lead to a substantial reduction in the demand for disposable plastic, and reduced use of materials and energy, with the consequent reduced environmental impacts. Container designers will take into account the fate of the container beyond the point of sale and consider the service the container provides. "Design for service" differs sharply from "design for disposal."

3. **Require producers to take back resins.** Get plastic manufacturers directly involved with plastic disposal and closing the material loop, which can stimulate them to consider the product's life cycle from cradle to grave. Make reprocessing easier by limiting the number of container types and shapes, using only one type of resin in each container, making collapsible containers, eliminating pigments, using water-dispersible adhesives for labels, and phasing out associated metals such as aluminum seals. Container and resin makers can help develop the reprocessing infrastructure by taking back plastic from consumers.

4. **Legislatively require recycled content.** Requiring that all containers be composed of a percentage of post-consumer material reduces the amount of virgin material consumed.

5. **Standardize labeling and inform the public.** The chasing arrows symbol on plastics is an example of an ambiguous and misleading label. Significantly different standardized labels for "recycled," "recyclable," and "made of plastic type X" must be developed.

sent out to be fixed. For things like burned-out compact fluorescent lightbulbs (CFLs contain mercury) or truly broken appliances, contact your municipality to find out if they're having an electronics drop-off drive anytime soon or, if not, what you're required to do with them. There are often very specific rules for how to curbside recycle something like a fridge, and CFLs can be brought to hazardous waste sites, or even taken to certain stores like Ikea for recycling. It sounds like more work than it is, especially if you're used to having someone just take your recyclables "away." But on a case-by-case basis, it's simple enough and, obviously, worthwhile.

tip If your town doesn't recycle them, plastic #5 yogurt cups can be sent to Preserve Products. The company turns them into toothbrushes, cutting boards, cups, and more. PreserveProducts.com/gimme5.

COMPOSTING

For biodegradable items to actually biodegrade in landfills, they need access to a basic combination of air, water, light, microbes, and enzymes. Landfill methane emissions are a result of the fact that landfills don't offer this access. Most are too tightly packed for biodegradable scraps to be exposed to such things, and so they sit, unbiodegraded, next to truly unbiodegradable items for years. In 1989, a garbage project out of the University of Arizona went into a landfill and discovered a legible newspaper from 1952, intact hot dogs, and an ear of corn (husks, too) mixed with material dated from 1971. Tragic but true. These findings are like poster children for why it's a good idea to keep even biodegradable items out of the landfill and aid the process yourself. Composting is truly win-win. It will drastically reduce your garbage output and give you

GARBAGE BAGS

Your nonrecyclable, noncompostable garbage should not end up in a trash bag containing added antimicrobial agents and hormone-disrupting synthetic fragrances meant to mask odors. Beware of any bags labeled "odor-neutralizing," "odor-blocking," "fresh, clean scent," or "scented." Instead, opt for ones made of recycled plastic (Seventh Generation—Seventh Generation.com) or ones that are biodegradable (Natural Value—NaturalValue.com and Bio Bags—BioBagUSA.com).

---

something valuable—nutrient-dense soil for your garden and house plants—in return from "trash." Seeing your atrophied garbage once you start composting is nothing short of miraculous—there's almost nothing in it! It's mind-boggling how much we collectively throw out that can simply, cheaply, and effectively be turned into good dirt. Once you've composted, you'll never go back.

Any kitchen trimmings that can't be made into stock should be composted, which you can easily do indoors or out. If you're lazy about going outside to your pile, you can collect your scraps in a stainless-steel container (some come with a built-in carbon filter for the possible smell that might arise) before your next trip to the compost. The Internet is overflowing with good how-to-compost resources, and the EPA maintains a solid compost page on its site—EPA.gov/waste/conserve/rrr/composting/index.htm. If you live in an apartment with no outdoor space, set up a worm bin (see sidebar, page 211), or splurge for a Nature Mill automatic indoor composter (it's been called the Cadillac of urban composters, and even takes meat); go to NatureMill.com for more information. I was given one for a milestone birthday. Best. Present. Ever. It takes some getting used to, but it works wonders and keeps my house plants, the trees outside my apartment building, and my friends' roof gardens happy. Some cities, like San Francisco and Toronto, are now collecting scraps for compost, and others have environmental groups or compost education nonprofits that take compostables. Ask around to find out who is doing this in your area. You can store scraps in your fridge or freezer during the week to take to collection sites on weekends.

STOCKPOSTING

Restaurants never waste a scrap; they can't afford to. But at home, we all do. It's alarming how much useable food we toss. Before composting, see what you can still use. Things like celery fronds, spinach stems, and the outer layers of onion can be used to make vegetable stock, for example. I call it stockposting. Keep a bowl in the fridge or a jar in the freezer to collect these odds and ends in, too, and when you have a full container (and the time) toss them on the stove in a pot of water with some seasoning. Strain it and store

---

WORM BINS

Indoor composting with worm boxes—aka vermicomposting—is a great way to deal with kitchen scraps, especially in an urban environment. Turn everything from orange peels and coffee grounds into "black gold" for your window-box organic herb garden and more. If you have kids, enlist their help—some adults are squeamish about worms, but children, for the most part, are not. Set it up yourself or attend a seminar. Some resources:

- *Worms Eat My Garbage* by Mary Applehof
- Kids.niehs.nih.gov/worms.htm
- RodaleInstitute.org
- VermiCultureNorthWest.com

---

the resulting broth in the fridge or freezer. What could be better than homemade veggie stock out of what you thought was nothing? For similar chicken stock, boil stockposting ingredients with a bound-for-the-garbage roast chicken carcass. It won't be as hearty as a traditional stock, but it does the trick to add flavor and liquid to grains, sauces, and more.

RESTAURANT RECYCLING
AND COMPOSTING

Restaurants aren't permitted by health departments to reuse leftovers the way people can at home, though some use untouched stale bread for French toast and crumbs, and clarify leftover butter. Other leftovers and scraps are sometimes given to services that feed people in need via organizations like City Harvest (City Harvest.org). They can also turn over their used grease and fry oil

---

TRASH-Y READING

If trash piques your interest, there are many life-cycle assessments on recycling versus tossing that are worth reading. Even the simplest web search reveals this to be as much of a hot-button topic as the local-versus-organic food debate. Here are some resources to help delve deeper into the trash pile.

- StoryOfStuff.org
- EcologyCenter.org
- ZeroWaste.org
- *Garbage Land: On the Secret Trail of Trash* by Elizabeth Royte
- *Rubbish! The Archaeology of Garbage* by William Rathje and Cullen Murphy
- *Cradle to Cradle: Remaking the Way We Make Things* by William McDonough and Michael Braungart

---

DEBORAH MADISON'S CARROT TOP SOUP

"Don't just throw them away," writes Deborah Madison in *Local Flavors: Cooking and Eating from America's Farmers' Markets*. "The tender tops that come with your carrots are delicious in soups." This recipe uses both tops and roots.

Serves 4

1 bunch (6 small to medium) carrots, the tops and the roots
2 tablespoons unsalted butter
3 tablespoons white rice
2 large leeks, white parts only
2 thyme or lemon thyme sprigs
2 tablespoons chopped dill, parsley, celery leaves, or lovage
Sea salt and freshly ground pepper
6 cups vegetable stock, light chicken stock, or water

1. Pull or pluck the lacy leaves of the carrot greens off their stems. You should have between 2 and 3 cups, loosely packed. Wash, then chop finely. Grate the carrots or, if you want a more refined-looking soup, finely chop them.

2. Melt the butter in a soup pot. Add the carrot tops and carrots, rice, leeks, thyme, and dill. Cook for several minutes, turning everything a few times, then season with 1½ teaspoons salt and add the stock. Bring to a boil and simmer until the rice is cooked, 16 to 18 minutes.

3. Taste for salt, season with pepper, and serve.

to a biodiesel company. (Tri-State Biodiesel does many of the res-taurants in my area—TriStateBiodiesel.com—it's a very cool busi-ness model.) Restaurants obviously can recycle. And they can also compost.

At Chez Panisse, in Berkeley, California, Alice Waters has the compost taken up to a produce purveyor's farm about an hour away. They bring back vegetables. Before the Stone Barns Center for Food and Agriculture existed, chef Dan Barber would take some of the Blue Hill kitchen scraps to New York's Union Square Green-market, where the Lower East Side Ecology Center (LESEcology Center.org) has been accepting dropoffs for composting since 1990. Now, Barber composts both his Blue Hill and Blue Hill at Stone Barns waste at Stone Barns. They have two composts—regular (just veggie scraps, plus things like eggshells and coffee grounds), and one for animal materials and scrapings from people's plates. They use the results at Stone Barns and even sell the regular stuff at their local Whole Foods.

Restaurants can also hire companies who come get scraps, though doing this depends on available cash and devotion. Chefs will tell you that training the staff to sort into separate composting bins as they work is an uphill battle, though it eventually becomes second nature. Which is exactly what compost is—nature given a second life. A fitting concept for every conscious kitchen.

ACKNOWLEDGMENTS

My endless and enormous gratitude to those who made it possible for me to write this book: Olli Chanoff and Aili Chanoff Zissu; Rica Allannic, Amy Hughes, David McCormick; Roger Zissu, Suzanne Zissu, Bill Meaders; and a bevy of babysitting Chanoffs (Molly, Lissu, David).

And thanks also to the following people and organizations for their much appreciated contributions to these pages, big and small (if I forgot you, I owe you a sustainable lunch):

Lloyd Alter
Jessica Applestone
Josh Applestone
Stephan Banville
Dan Barber
Emily Beretta
Lelia Cafaro
Judy Carmichael
Rachel Chanoff
Mary Cleaver
Coffee
Doris Cooper
Consumers Union/*Consumer Reports*
Corrina
Beck Cowles
Deirdre Dolan
Environmental Defense Fund
Environmental Working Group
Sally Fallon
Eve Felder
Tim Fitzgerald
Ben Ford
Lisa Frack
Steve Gold
Courtney Greenhalgh
Taras Grescoe
Joan Gussow

Irene Hamburger
Shannon Hayes
Health Canada
Alexandra Jacobs
Deb Kavakos
Barbara Kingsolver
Emeril Lagasse
Jenny Lefcourt
Don Lewis
Jean Lynch
Deborah Madison
Emily Main
Jack Mazzola
Marisa McDonald
Jeff Moyers
Natural Resources Defense Fund
Marion Nestle
Paul Novack
Meaghan O'Neill
Max Oswald
Laura Pagano
Donna Passannante
Mindy Pennybacker
Ashley Phillips
Nina Planck
Michael Pollan
Jenny Powers

Marysarah Quinn
Daniel Sauer
Dan Shapley
Cora Sita
Heather Reichardt
Elizabeth Rendfleisch
Liz Scatena
Jennifer Sass
Lauren Shakely
Sam Simon
Sustainable Table
TheDailyGreen.com
The Ecology Center
Michelle Terrebonne
Amy Topel
Treehugger.com
Kate Tyler
Alice Waters
Christina Wang
Wine
Wendy J. Wintman
Martin Wolf
Malia Wollan
Tricia Wygal
Yoga
Jonathan Zearfoss
Leesa Zissu

CREDITS

Grateful acknowledgment is made to the following for permission
to print previously published or new material:

37 Sautéed Kale as first seen on an episode of *Emeril Green* television show.
    Copyright © 2008 Emeril Lagasse. All rights reserved. Reprinted with
    permission.
45 The Environmental Working Group: All mentions of their research,
    including but not limited to the "Dirty Dozen" and "Clean Fifteen," and
    lists and quotes from their "Bottled Water Report," are reprinted with
    permission.
50 Consumers Union: The information in the labels primer is Copyright
    © 2009 by Consumers Union of U.S., Inc. Yonkers, NY 10703-
    1057, a nonprofit organization. Reprinted with permission from
    GreenerChoices.org for educational purposes only. No commercial use
    or reproduction permitted. GreenerChoices.org; ConsumerReports.org.
76 NewTrends Publishing: Yogurt recipe from *Nourishing Traditions:
    The Cookbook that Challenges Politically Correct Nutrition and
    the Diet Dictocrats* by Sally Fallon with Mary G. Enig, Ph.D.
    Copyright © NewTrends Publishing. Reprinted with permission.
    (NewTrendsPublishing,com)
90 Environmental Defense Fund: "Seafood Selector." Copyright © 2009
    Environmental Defense Fund. Reprinted with permission. (EDF.org/
    seafood)

93 Michael Pollan: salmon recipe printed with permission.

126–27 HarperCollins Publishers and Faber and Faber Ltd.: "Friday Night Pizza" from *Animal, Vegetable, Miracle* by Barbara Kingsolver with Steven L. Hopp and Camille Kingsolver, copyright © 2007 by Barbara Kingsolver, Stephen L. Hopp, and Camille Kingsolver. Reprinted by permission of HarperCollins Publishers and Faber and Faber Ltd.

181 Health Canada: "It's Your Health: Microwave Ovens and Food Safety" by Health Canada, July 2005. Reproduced by permission of the Minister of Public Works and Government Services Canada, 2009.

190–91 Shannon Hayes: Grilled steak recipe from *The Farmer and the Grill: A Guide to Grilling, Barbecuing, and Spit-Roasting Grassfed Meat, and for Saving the Planet, One Bite at a Time* by Shannon Hayes. Copyright © Shannon Hayes. Reprinted with permission. (GrassFedCooking.com)

198 Mindy Pennybacker and National Geographic Society: "What Cleaning-Product Ingredients to Avoid," The Green Guide, March 1, 2006. Reprinted with permission by Mindy Pennybacker (GreenerPenny.com) and National Geographic Society.

208 The Ecology Center: "Five Strategies to Reduce the Environmental Impact of Plastics." Copyright © The Ecology Center. Reprinted with permission. (EcologyCenter.org)

213 Broadway Books: "Carrot Top Soup" recipe from *Local Flavors: Cooking and Eating From America's Farmers' Markets* by Deborah Madison. Copyright © 2002 by Deborah Madison. Used by permission of Broadway Books, a division of Random House, Inc.

INDEX

agribusiness, defined, 14
aluminum: in baking powder, 132; baking
    sheets, 151; cans *vs.* glass bottles, 120; as
    foil, 192; pots and pans, 149
ammonia, 198
animals, grass-fed, 11, 52, 53, 54, 55, 59,
    60–61, 205
antibiotics, in meat, 14, 21, 56–57
apples, 43, 44
Applestone, Jessica, 52, 58–61, 66
appliances, 170–72
aquaculture, 81
arsenic, in poultry feed, 57
artificial sweeteners, 128

bakeware, 150–52
baking powder, 132
bananas, 33, 45–47, 107, 122, 123
barbecues, *see* grilling
Barber, Dan, 34–35, 61, 62, 94, 214
barramundi, 91
beef, grass-fed, 11, 49, 52
beer, 117–20
bees, 131
bibs, safe, 165
biodynamic farming, 15, 112–13
bison meat, 61
bisphenol-A (BPA), 83, 120, 124, 155,
    156–57, 183
bivalves, 92
black pepper, 133
bleach, 10, 64, 151, 163, 195, 196, 197,
    198
Blue Ocean Institute, 86, 89, 91
bottled water, 96–100

BPA (bisphenol-A), 83, 120, 124, 155,
    156–57, 183
bread, 125, 128
Brita, 101
brown sugar, 129–30
buffalo meat, 61
bulk, buying in, 160, 204
butter, 77, 128, 144

cadmium, 164
CAFO (concentrated animal feeding
    operation), defined, 16
candles, 167–68
canned food, 83, 124
canola oil, 138
carbon footprint: about, 30–31; calculating
    for wine, 114–16; and country-of-origin
    labels, 30; defined, 15; and food miles,
    17, 30–31; impact of buying organic
    food products, 28; information
    resources, 32; orange juice example,
    104
carrot top soup, Deborah Madison's recipe,
    213
carryout containers, 147, 183, 207
cast iron: bakeware, 150; caring for pans,
    144; enamel-coated pans, 145; pan
    overview, 143–44
caterers, 193
caulk, 201
Center for Environmental Health (CEH),
    102
Certified Humane label, 51–52
certified organic, defined, 15
charcoal grills, 187, 189–91